8D Dtc

D1265177

CARVING IN WOOD

CARVING IN WOOD

A Personal Approach to an Old Craft

DAVID GREEN

LONDON
VICTOR GOLLANCZ LTD
in association with Peter Crawley
1981

ISBN 0 575 02964 1

Text printed in Great Britain by
BAS Printers Limited, Over Wallop, Hampshire
Plates printed in Great Britain by
W S Cowell Ltd, Ipswich

To Jonathan

ACKNOWLEDGEMENTS

This book grew out of conversations with my friend Peter Crawley and for his enthusiastic encouragement at all stages during the writing and illustrating I am especially grateful. When the manuscript was completed to our joint satisfaction the production and publication was carried out by Victor Gollancz Ltd, the staff of which have been equally helpful and pleasing to work with. In particular I should like to express my appreciation of the kindness of David Burnett, Stephen Bray and Nellie Flexner.

Although I took the colour photographs myself I am grateful for the advice and help of Angela Coombes, Ewen Wannop, Raymond Williams and also the efficient service provided by Colour Processing Laboratory Ltd of Bristol. Karen Hunt and Tom Barnard are thanked for processing black and white photographs which served as bases for some of the drawings. Further information for some of the drawings in Chapter Two was obtained from *The Complete Book of Tools* (Jackson and Day) and the *Dictionary of Tools* (Salaman), details of which will be found in the Bibliography. Acknowledgement is also made of information on gouges obtained from Tiranti's catalogue for the Table on page 44. The address of this firm is given in the List of Suppliers.

Finally to John Repper I am indebted for help with blacksmithery; to Robert Curry for his help with tools long before the book was ever considered; to my daughter Susan for all the typing and some of the decorative work on the examples illustrated in colour; to Jonathan for his ship; to Ronald Parsons for his decorative work and interest, to Reg Beint for timber and to Stiles and Stiles Ltd of Corsham for occasional photocopying.

CONTENTS

(continued overleaf)

List of Illustrations in Text

(continued overleaf)

List of Colour Plates

Following page 46

1. The 'great oval dish' described in Chapter One.
2. Mallet turned from a discarded 'wood' by Geoffrey Hawkins and handmade gouge.

Following page 70

3. The author's favourite gouges for bowlmaking.
4. Three similar bowls in different stages showing at the simplest level the evolution of the three-dimensional qualities of disappearing surfaces and space underneath.

Following page 106

5. Three bowls with edges decorated by a pyrographic needle.
6. Two small bowls in oiled and burnished elm.
7. Carving the interior of a bowl in horsechestnut.
8. Small carving in a mahogany by the author.

PREFACE

In this short book I want to share with readers some of the excitement and satisfaction I have had over the last few years from carving wood. This is a remarkably simple pastime as it requires little space, comparatively few tools and involves as much muscular activity as intellectual. The practical requirements are indeed so minimal that it is possible to make a beginning as soon as a chisel and piece of wood have been found. The back door step can serve as a bench and another billet of wood as a mallet—with nothing more the first job can be seen right through to the finish. But readers will want to launch out beyond this stage and will have therefore to be prepared to spend a pound or two now and again; not much and only very rarely in two figures.

Those who know that I have spent most of my professional life teaching and writing about ceramics will wonder what I am about, so let me put the record straight. My grandfather was a wheelwright and my father a potter and designer at Wedgwoods. He left the industry to become principal of an art school in 1929, so that I grew up in this mixed environment of the arts and crafts with a variety of interesting potters, painters, sculptors, collectors and musicians to talk to. Before my quarter century was up I had therefore acquired considerable experience in the arts and had even begun on the task of making a success as a painter with frequent contributions to exhibitions in London and elsewhere. My hereditary interest in pottery displaced everything else when the opportunity to establish a new department for this craft at Carlisle College of Art was offered to me in 1959 and it has remained at the forefront of my teaching activities ever since.

However, there has always been at the back of my mind the memory of a youthful summer in a Devon garden chipping away at some pieces of stone from a bombed site under the inspiring guidance of the sculptor

13

John Skeaping, Barbara Hepworth's first husband and at the time a close friend of Henry Moore. The thump thump of the hammer, the ring of the chisels, and the excitement of the figures emerging from their blocks of tough resistant material out there in the sunshine has never really diminished. My modest collection of masons' tools has been lovingly preserved in case the opportunity should ever arise again, but stone carving is a difficult business to organise as it really does require a separate workshop, as well as a great deal of time, if anything much is to be achieved. Neither has ever been available to me, and, as nothing was lacking in fulfilment from my other activities, the pressure to establish the facilities for a return to this work has never been there.

Then, one day, out with the children and the dog, I stumbled across a large boss of timber cut from a diseased elm. Instantly I saw inside the wood a great oval dish and although I had never before carved in wood

'I saw inside the wood a great oval dish'

(and had few tools for the work) the desire to smash this bowl out was too strong to resist. The heavy piece of wood was dragged home and as soon as there was breath in my body again the task was begun. What follows in these chapters is an account of how the difficulties were steadily overcome together with a summary of what was learned about tools and timber during several years of finding out the hard way.

We do appear to set far too much store by specialisation or professionalism. There is rarely very much in any job that a determined outsider cannot master in time, and, although his efforts may not be executed with the swift assurance of those who have been at the work all their lives, the outsider may well be bringing in to the work a wider vision and more feeling. There is certainly nothing in the craft of the woodcarver to deter anyone and, one suspects, plenty to be brought in. For a long time the craft seems to have been substantially reproductive—looking back at old models of furniture or the figure—and only rarely does the work appear to be carried out with renewed joy or any real feeling for tactile sculptural qualities. Here there is another side of the business for us to look at in these pages, in reality more important than the techniques.

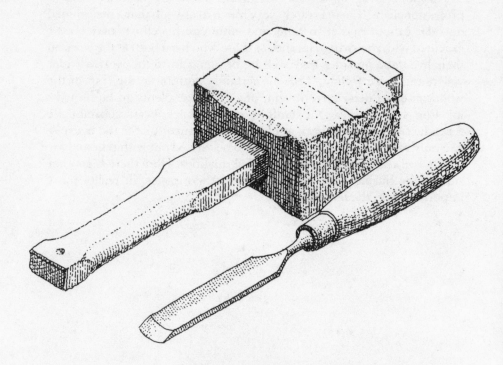

Traditional carpenter's beechwood mallet and
firmer gouge with the bevel on the inside.

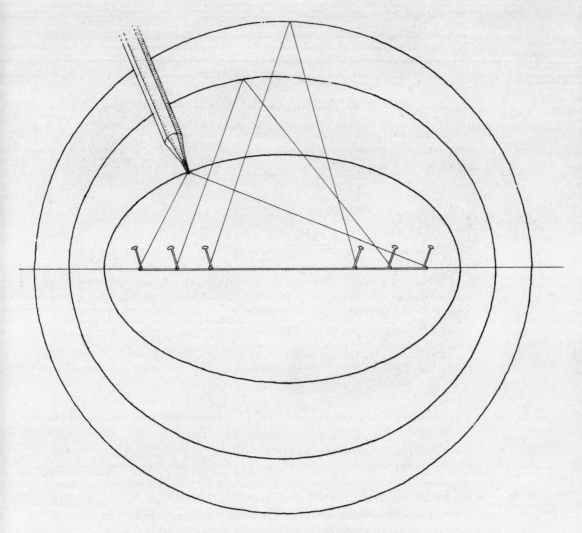

To draw an oval accurately, set two nails several inches
apart and tie a loop of string loosely around them. A pencil
inserted in this loop will describe a perfect oval when the
string is stretched tight. The shorter the distance between
the nails the nearer the oval will approach a circular shape.

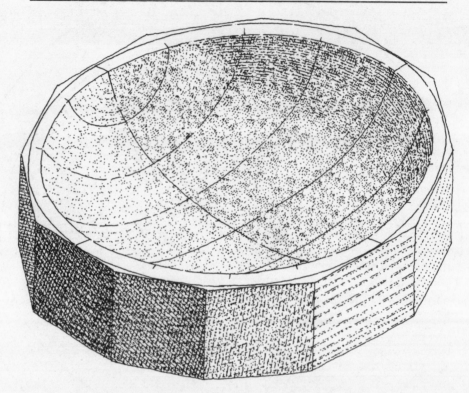

'. . . I marked out a series of broad bands along the main axis of the oval and maintained a direction of cutting within these.'

it easy to chisel down to a flat surface. The bottom was then planed to a smooth finish with equal ease as the piece was heavy enough to stay still without stops or clamps.

From this point the hollowing of the inside proceeded with pleasure and without difficulty until it became necessary to give thought to the direction of the rather deep marks the gouge was making. In the early stages these marks were distinctly untidy and in attempting to radiate them from a central point I not only ran into difficulties with some parts of the grain but also could not cope satisfactorily with the meeting point at the bottom. It was obvious that a selection of bent gouges with shallow curvatures would make life very much easier, but as anything of this nature seemed unobtainable I marked out a series of broad bands along the long axis of the oval and maintained a direction of cutting within these. The effect was a swooping movement through the dish which, as it did not appear to interfere with the form, seemed a reasonable compromise.

Finishing the inside revealed that the toughness of the wood varied considerably from one part to another. One end was like iron, but the sides, where the natural curvature of the outer surface hardly required adjusting to match the inside, were quite soft. This soft wood was of course the outer layer or 'sapwood' of the tree, and, as I discovered later, one of the characteristics of elm wood is that it is usable almost to the bark as it hardens on drying. But the tough end was the thickest and on turning the bowl over to shape the back it was evident that the removal of the surplus wood here—by now thoroughly dry—was going to be a lengthy task. There was also the problem of marking out an accurate base area to correspond with the rim as the back was completely irregular.

The work had not, though, proceeded continuously. If I remember correctly, the making of this dish took up the free hours throughout one whole term as well as the vacations at either end, so that it was in the intervals between the working sessions that all the problems like the marking out of the base or the direction of the gouge marks on the inside were solved in my mind—mostly on journeys to work.

Luckily the paper template had been kept and on it was already marked the line of the long axis of the oval. From the centre of this line the points of the short axis on the rim could be found with a set square and these four points marked on the wood by replacing the template in its original position. The surplus wood was then sawn and planed away from the outer edge so that the dish assumed its final shape from the top view. The four ends of the axis were then marked down the sides a little so that they were visible when the dish was turned over. It was now a simple matter to stretch strings from one mark to the other across the irregular back and to mark out on the flat base area the lines of these two axes. A smaller oval was then drawn with string and pins which

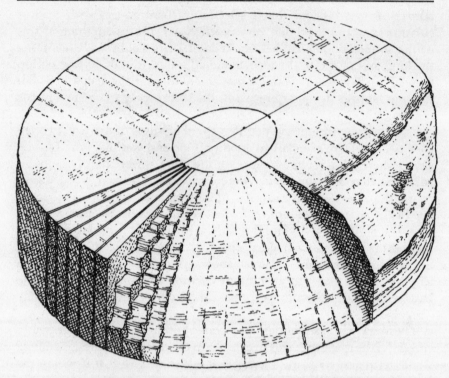

'. . . I made a series of radiating saw cuts across the form
. . . and proceeded to chip the wood away between these
cuts with a flat chisel.'

corresponded in shape reasonably accurately with the rim.

Now, as the gouge seemed exceptionally slow in removing the surplus
wood from the back, I made a series of radiating saw cuts across the form
at intervals of about one inch and proceeded to chip the wood away
between these cuts with a flat chisel. Estimating the curvature between
rim and base for these saw cuts did not prove difficult and the form of the
dish began to emerge quite quickly. The surface was finished with a
plane which again did not prove a difficult operation as the dish was large
enough for me to sit on whilst working across the curvature down to a
part of the rim which was projected over the edge of the bench. Finally

the outer edge of the rim was finished with a small bevel and the surface polished with fine sand and flour papers.

As the work rushed towards completion the excitement gained momentum. With each stroke of the plane new areas of grain pattern were brought into focus and the surface began to have meaning in relation to the form. For the first time the weight of the dish began to make sense and the thickness to feel logical in relation to the rim. And it sounded different—alive instead of dull. It sprang into my hands and my satisfaction was complete when I discovered that others responded to it in the same way. I had made a dish which actually demanded to be picked up!

Chapter Two

THE GOURMAND AND THE CHEF

My delight at having made a bowl that 'sprang into my hands' and 'sounded alive' suggests that I had hoped to imbue this object with some kind of vital force. Does this seem a little unnecessary, even a little pretentious, for an object that can hardly be described as anything more than a common fruit bowl? I don't think so, but to explain why I shall have to try to put into words what I feel to be the essence of a three-dimensional craft like bowlcarving, for there is very definitely another aspect of the business besides the pleasure involved in the making.

This other side is to do with communication between the craftsman and the user of his products. In the 'fine arts'—painting, sculpture, music, literature etc.—there is a tangible transfer of ideas and emotions, which are not generally difficult to isolate, between the artist and his public. In music, of course, the emotional response is aroused by the aural sense; in painting and many other arts the method of transfer is through vision. Only in sculpture and architecture (as distinct from building!) is the visual connection between the artist and the spectator supported by an actual physical link, the sense of touch, or of experiencing solid volumes and empty spaces around which the spectator's whole body is drawn, just as the sculptor's was during the original process of making or the architect had planned it should be.

Now the sense of touch and the compulsion to explore solid and empty volumes by moving the whole body are very powerful and much misunderstood emotional channels for an artist to employ. They are the very ones with which we are concerned here. At birth they are the most highly developed of our senses, capable of arousing extremes of pleasure or distaste, but as life goes on they become jaded by wholetime employment throughout every moment of our waking hours. Our hands are forever in contact with something and our feet continually

24

steering us in one direction or another for entirely mundane purposes. To wake up these deadened and long since forgotten senses is an exceptionally challenging task which the craftsman is duty-bound to take on if he expects to be considered an artist.

By suggesting that these senses are misunderstood and largely forgotten I am unfortunately indulging in criticism of the general level of craftwork to be seen in shops, exhibitions or our art teaching institutions, in particular in pottery, the very craft where one would expect the hands to become most involved. It is in fact incredibly difficult to get many students to feel objects with their hands; PLEASE DO NOT TOUCH is *de rigueur* throughout the art world, and, while our visual senses are overfed with a surfeit of pictures, films, T.V., illustrated books, and magazines, the sense of touch is starved and frustrated. Almost every object of merit from past generations is shut away behind glass and when artists of repute in other media turn to the crafts it is as often as not to the colourful or decorative aspects, not the tactile, that they lend their weight. Can we wonder, therefore, that young students have difficulty in understanding this side of their work and seek to make up for its lack by indulging in a veritable rat race for colour, surface pattern, texture and visual gimmickry?

Well, behind all the arts is a grammar or a set of more or less definable abstract rules, or conventions, which an artist can use as an aid towards assembling his ideas and getting them across to others. In sculpture we can very easily identify one quite fundamental rule or grammatical trick of this kind for making observers more conscious than normal of the third dimension and therefore more likely to respond to tactile values.* This can be described as the provision of at least one surface at every viewpoint which cannot be seen in its entirety but disappears from view round to the far side. Its disappearance enhances the solidity of an object by leading the eye of the observer round the form and so making him conscious of the existence of a side he cannot see from where he is standing at the moment.

*This useful term was introduced into the language of art criticism by Bernard Berenson in his famous study of *The Florentine Painters of the Renaissance* which was first published in 1896. This short essay, only 94 small pages with one plate, was the first of its kind and made an immediate and lasting impact on the art world. The book can still be purchased in modern illustrated editions.

If his curiosity is sufficiently aroused, the observer is impelled to either *move* his body round the object to find out what happens to this surface, or, if the object is small enough, to pick it up and to turn it around in his hands.

Here, then is the first step towards the creation of 'vital force' and it follows that this effect of 'movement' can be achieved in varying degrees. A coloured or textured band on an otherwise uninteresting form—the old barbers' pole idea—will achieve very little movement on the part of the spectator, whereas an organised form, of which the disappearing surface represents the outer extremity of one of its parts, can be quite effective. If all the forms—and the empty spaces between or around them— contribute to the effect any sensitive observer is immediately taken over and led, disarmed and unresisting, in the intended direction.

When the observer has been taken over in this way he can be fed very powerfully with any other emotive ideas the sculptor is intending to convey, although many sculptors during the last half century have found that the take over of the observer's aesthetic responses in this abstract way, as in music, can sometimes be sufficiently satisfying without any additional political, religious or other emotional ideas associated with the figurative arts.

Looking at bowls for a while as forms, not vessels, we can begin to see immediately how movement can be created and a simple com- municational link established between the maker and the user. The shape of the inner surface is important, but far more so is the relationship of the empty cavity this surface contains to the outer caves beneath the bowl, because between these two volumes of space lies the solid form of the shell. As soon as an observer sees the bowl his eyes begin to assess its form from the shape of these cavities. Most of the interior is likely to be visible enough for the assessments to be completed at a glance, but this can never be so with the outside where the surface rapidly disappears from view. His hands may reach out to explore this lower volume of space, but before they do so the character of the rim of the shell will have caught his eye. This is all important because the rim gives the observer the first indication of what he is likely to experience by touch. It will give an idea of weight by its thickness, but, more so, it will begin to show how the inner and outer surfaces of the bowl relate together.

If the rim of the bowl is flat—as it inevitably was at one stage during the making, when the inner cavity had first been carved out—the eye will be able to see its full extent around the perimeter of the bowl, but if the rim is moulded in some way this can never be so. Only at the front will the full extent be visible; just over half way round some surfaces of the rim will begin to disappear from view, while others—those tipped inwards towards the bowl—will become more evident.

At the very simplest level these three-dimensional qualities can be seen to develop in Plate 4 showing three stages in the making of a shallow dish. In reality the effect is more powerful because our vision is stereoscopic, whereas that of the camera is not.

There are, of course dozens of shapes the plunging interior of a bowl can be given and many more possibilities for the exterior, to say nothing of the infinite variety of connecting rim forms. There will, however, be little choice about the shape of the first interior we carve; it will arrive from the struggle to master our possibly inadequate tools and will, in general, be dictated by the size and thickness of timber at our disposal.

It is, then, in the choice of a form for the back and the rim that we first begin to exercise our own tactile senses and the bowl will need handling and looking at very frequently as the work progresses. Here is part of the satisfaction of this work; the emerging dish is on the bench for days, possibly weeks, and our critical faculties run over its form every time we pass, even if we have not the time to stop and do anything to it. The form lingers in our minds while we are away from it and the feel of it is in our fingers. The next development is considered . . .

Notice too the changing effect of light. The strong line of shadow cast inside by clear sunlight is very revealing about the character of the inner curvature and can show deformities which were not seen in other lights. The play of light and shadow over the rim form is vital too and one of the chief criticisms of the flat rim—often seen by the way—is the fact that there is no changing play of light and shadow over it at all. But strong sunlight is not always the best for working in or seeing forms. The quieter light of an English grey can be much more revealing.

On the subject of training our tactile senses Henry Moore has this to say:

We all think we see three-dimensional form—but we don't. People have to be trained to comprehend spaces in order to understand the shape of something. Great draughtsmen such as Rembrandt, Michelangelo or Rubens could each draw three-dimensional form. Rembrandt in his late self portraits could make the nose have the right projection in front of the cheeks, and the forehead the right distance in front of the eyes. He could do this to a great extent as a young man, but he did it better and better as he got older. Now if a genius takes all that time to see form and learn how to represent it completely, the average person cannot expect to understand it fully. He may get a general idea, but no more.

(John Hedgecoe, *Henry Moore*, Nelson, London, 1968, page 65)

And it is surprising how quickly one gets beyond the 'general idea' when one's hands and mind are involved in the making! In this respect my 'great oval dish', which delighted me when it was first made, is, I find, no longer so satisfying. The weight is not right and the distribution uneven. There are many places on the outside where more timber could be removed with benefit and I am unsure about the appropriateness of the gouged texture within. My second and third bowls, upon which I attempted to use a bandsaw with tilted bed for removing waste wood from the exterior, were later judged to be complete failures. One was recarved but the other was taken over by my son who cut a section out of the middle to make the hull of a medieval warship!

It is amazing how the removal of a little bulk—perhaps less than a millimetre of thickness—on a curved surface can change the nature of a form and alter its tactile quality. Trained hands are peculiarly responsive, and, in this context, I remember once meeting a specialist instrument maker who told me that his fingers were more reliable to him than the most sensitive measuring device a modern industry could provide. With his fingers in top form he was aware of variations of thickness in thin metal plates of very much less than one thousandth of an inch, although after a fortnight's holiday his sensitivity in this respect required refurbishing.

Another example concerns a highly intelligent mature student who came into a pottery class to savour the feel of a craft as a contrast to the

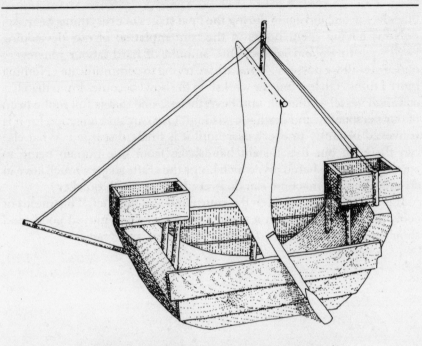

Medieval warship made by a boy from the
centre section of a discarded bowl.

literature and music which had preoccupied his life so far. He brought
with him a considerable enthusiasm and a rugged sense of form in keeping
with his stature, but, for several hours one day, he floundered
completely in smoothing the surface of a lump of clay ready for casting
as a dish mould. When I finally took over the job myself he suddenly
exclaimed 'Ah, smooth! I've never felt a surface like that before'. His
fingers had, of course, often been in contact with the far 'smoother'
surfaces of, for instance, polished furniture, but never before had the
sensation been consciously routed from his fingers to his brain. He had
been mistaking the high burnish that he could *see* he had achieved in
isolated areas for the continuity of the whole form which is necessary for
an object to *feel* smooth. The degree of polish—or texture—achieved on
the actual surface is a different matter altogether as we shall discover for

ourselves again and again during the final stages of everything we make.

Now, having spent hours in the contemplation of our developing bowl sculpture—and an immense amount of hard labour plus every ounce of skill we possess—what are we trying to communicate? Nothing more I think. On leaving our workshop the bowl becomes immediately a common vessel or utensil, but, nevertheless, one that is full to the brim of our personality and aesthetic wisdom. Our care and affection for it is conveyed instantly to every user until it is finaly discarded. What else can there be but this distant handshake from one human being to another, and the shared joy, which keeps the crafts so very much alive in an age when the machine can do everything so much quicker?

It is like the bond between the gourmand and the chef. The fine art of cooking would die within a week if all those who enjoyed good food should suddenly turn to a diet of tinned beans and spam!

Chapter Three

TOOLS

The minimal requirements for wood carving suggested in the Preface—one chisel and a billet of wood for a mallet—would not, of course, satisfy anyone for long. The work on the back doorstep would be uncomfortable and many of our ideas would be entirely frustrated. Frustration has, though, always been the mother of invention. The artist who has reached this limit with his existing tools understands their limitation only too well and has in his mind a shrewd idea of what is required to enable him to move on. He is in a much stronger position than the beginner pitched into a fully equipped workshop, for such a person understands nothing and yet can achieve everything. Most of us will start somewhere between these two extremes and soon be devising better ways of coping with the work on hand. Here are some of my experiences and findings with regard to tools.

MACHINE TOOLS

The kind friend who reground the bevel of my firmer gouge told me that he would remove the wood from the interior of a bowl shape by drilling rings of large holes and would only use a gouge for the final shaping. On my way home I therefore bought the largest flat bit for an electric drill that could be found and set about the work as he suggested. For a few moments the slivers of wood flew about very satisfactorily, but rapidly the wet elm took the edge off the bit and, as the drill strained on noisily, progress with the second and third holes became slower and slower. An old bit in my brace did better and no machine tools have been employed in the actual shaping of my work since this first day. Now that I am properly equipped with hand tools it is not easy to see how any could help so I am spared the noise and vibration!

Removing surplus timber from the outside—cutting away the logs as

31

I still call it—is a different matter and a task that I would happily mechanise if the opportunity arose. Unfortunately the really tedious work of this kind on hardwoods over 4 inches* in thickness is well beyond the small or medium sized bandsaws and anything more robust would not only be expensive but would require substantial electrical installation. Below 4 inches a good tree saw (30 inches) is quite effective, although I do borrow a bandsaw when a number of small pieces of work have been planned out in advance.

SAWS

While we are on the subject of saws I have found a selection of them speeds the chore of removing surplus timber by hand. There is no such thing as a universal saw, for the tooth shape necessary for cutting across the grain of wood is different from that required for cutting along it.

The Romans seem to have contributed most to early saw design by putting the soft metals available to them under tension from a bent wooden frame or with twine across the opposite ends of a wooden H frame. They also introduced rake to the teeth and bending them

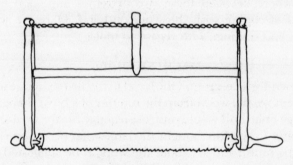

Traditional bow saw.

outwards in alternate directions—setting—to make a cut or 'kerf' wider than the blade itself to reduce sticking. By medieval times the manufacture of iron had been sufficiently improved for it to be possible to produce saws which were pushed into the wood, rather than pulled towards the operator in order to avoid bending. The final versions of

*One inch = 25.4 mm (approximately 2.5 cm).

modern saws emerged during the eighteenth and nineteenth centuries, although improvements in steels—especially with regard to rust proofing and durability—are still being made.

In a good modern saw—and there are plenty about which do not come into this category—tension is acquired in the metal itself by expanding the centre part of the blade during the tempering process. The blade is also subtly tapered in thickness away from the cutting edge by grinding in a radial fashion from the front corner.

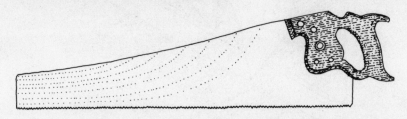

Modern cross-cut saw showing radial grinding.

For convenience the teeth of most saws are equilateral triangles to correspond with the shape of three-sided sharpening files. In a saw designed for cutting across the grain of timber, the rake of the triangular teeth is established by tilting them about 16° off the vertical so that the forward slope is at an angle of 14° while the rear slope is at 46°. Only the top half of each tooth is set, otherwise they would be weakened at the root, and the teeth are bevelled on their inner faces so that their tips perform like two rows of sharp points cutting through the fibres on either side of the kerf. The short length of fibre left between these two cuts then powders away as sawdust. (*See overleaf*)

The teeth of a rip saw used for cutting with the grain are again equilateral, raked with the leading edge at about 3° from the vertical and the back at 57°. The rip saw is set like the cross-cut but the teeth are sharpened straight across without bevels to act like so many narrow chisels. (*See overleaf*)

Most rip saws have about five teeth to the inch, but cross cuts vary between six and ten. Saws with the larger teeth are used on softwoods, where there is less resistance, and with the smaller ones on hardwoods. A general purpose saw will have about eight teeth to the inch.

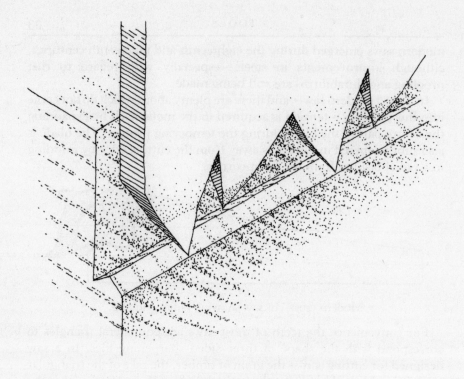

The action of cross-cut saw teeth.

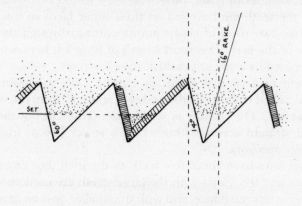

The angles of cross-cut saw teeth.

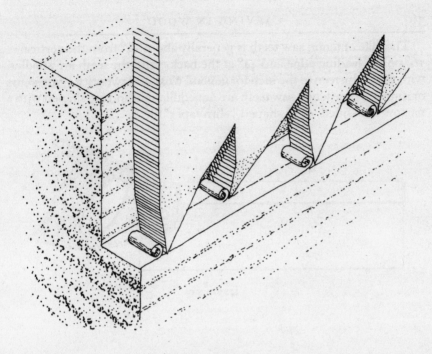

The action of rip-saw teeth.

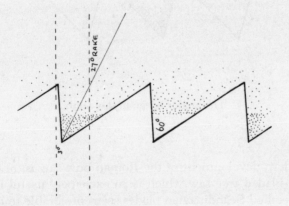

The angles of rip-saw teeth.

The rake of tenon saw teeth is generally about 14° from the vertical—16° on the leading edge and 44° at the back—and the teeth are smaller, with about thirteen to the inch for general work and twenty for fine joints or mitres. Some tenon saw teeth are not equilateral and are shaped with a narrow two-sided, or V shaped, 'slim taper' file.

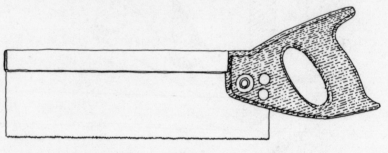

Tenon saw.

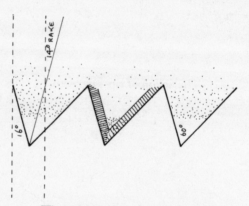

The angles of tenon saw teeth.

The modern development of the Roman bow saw is, of course, the replaceable-bladed tree saw which is an extremely useful implement. The even-teethed Scandinavian blades seem preferable to the English pattern which consists of groups of teeth separated by deep furrows for work of this kind. Better still, is a 'farmers' saw' which is similar to a rip saw but with large, easily sharpened, 'M' shaped teeth.

On every modern workbench there should be a specially designed sheet saw to obviate the need to use any others on such ruinous materials as chip board, hardboard or formica.

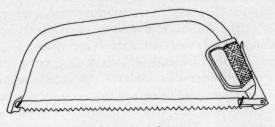

Modern tree or log saw.

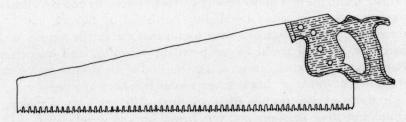

Farmers' saw.

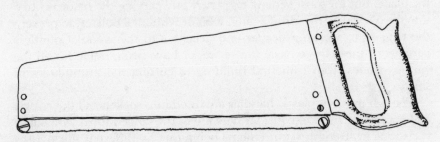

Modern sheet saw.

CHISELS AND GOUGES

Some amazing carvings were produced before the first metal was discovered, and, though archaeologists may be interested in finding out how flint microliths were used, it is doubtful whether any readers of this book would contemplate much in the way of woodcarving before they had acquired at least one tool with a steel cutting edge!

When the existence of metals did come to light in the Near East sometime during the fifth millennium B.C. the chisel was among the first implements to be made, and its spread from community to community throughout Europe, Asia and Africa is regarded as an important turning point in development. The first chisels were of course made from copper, but these were replaced during the third millennium B.C. by bronze and in the first millennium by wrought iron. By 700 B.C. the fact that wrought iron could be slightly hardened by heating had been discovered and the Romans soon found that the brittle nature of the hardened material could be tempered by reheating and quenching. Refinements quickly followed and by the end of the Roman era most of the different forms of chisels in use to-day had been evolved.

In terms of construction there are three different ways of making a chisel. For stone masonry and very heavy work in wood—such as ship or wagon building—the blade and handle of the tools are cast in one piece. For less heavy work a wooden handle is fitted into a socket cast on the blade, but for most general carpentry and carving the blade is fitted into the handle by means of a tang, with or without a bolster, to prevent the tang from working deeper and deeper into the wood. Countless variants of these three basic forms are, or have been, made for all the various trades from cathedral building to cutting the buttonholes in shirts.

Though modern plastic handles are fitted into sockets, all the chisels and gouges we need to consider here are of the tanged form with slight variations in strength requirements being met by different thicknesses and shaping of the blade.

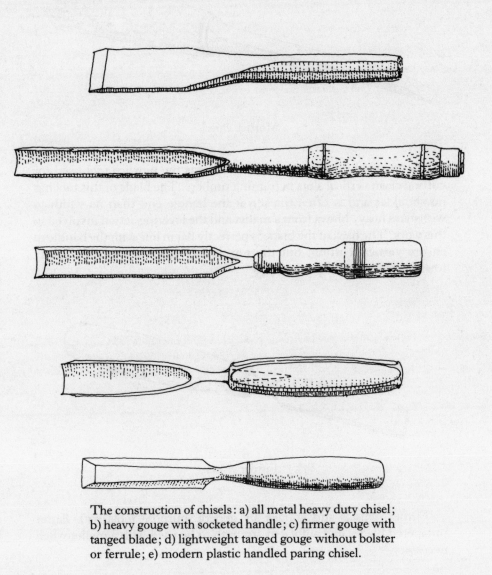

The construction of chisels: a) all metal heavy duty chisel;
b) heavy gouge with socketed handle; c) firmer gouge with
tanged blade; d) lightweight tanged gouge without bolster
or ferrule; e) modern plastic handled paring chisel.

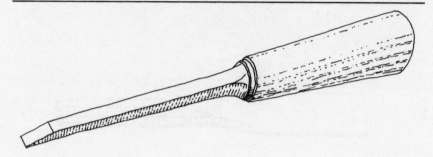

Mortice chisel.

The toughest chisel in a carpenter's kit is the mortice tool used for cutting clean vertical slots in framing timbers. The blade of this tool has no shoulder and is often thicker at the handle end than its width to withstand heavy blows from a mallet and the levering action involved in this work. The back of the blade is perfectly flat in line with the handle to ensure vertical cutting, but the top surface generally tapers slightly towards the bevelled cutting edge.

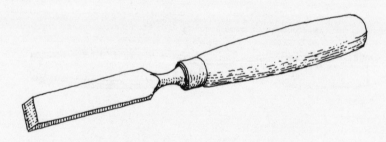

Firmer chisel.

'Firmer' chisels and gouges are general purpose tools with flatter untapered blades and sufficient strength to be used with a mallet when necessary.

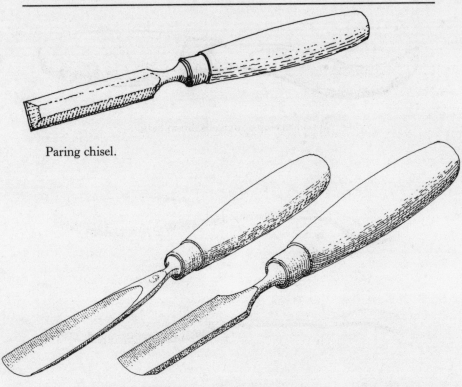

Paring chisel.

Woodcarving and firmer gouges.

Finally, a carpenter will carry a range of 'paring' chisels which have thinnish blades bevelled down the length of each side and with perfectly flat backs. These tools are used without mallets for slicing away the final shavings of halving joints or tenons.

As we have seen already in Chapter One, the bevel of the cutting edge in firmer gouges—the cannel as it is called—can be on the back (out-cannelled) or the front (in-cannelled) according to whether the tool is intended to cut vertically into the wood or with a gentle hollowing action, and, although these tools can be obtained in several widths, the cross-sections do not vary. The firmer gouge is a substantial tool but it does not remove wood rapidly and is of little use to the carver.

Woodcarving gouge—'salmon bend'.

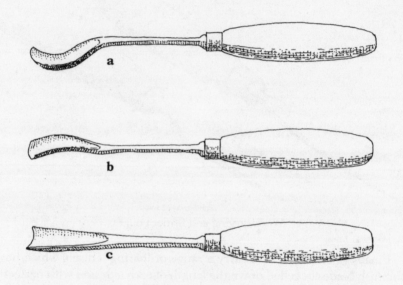

Woodcarving gouges: a) front bent; b) back bent; c) fishtail.

Woodcarving gouges are entirely different in shape, the blades being tapered in thickness towards the cutting edge and in width towards the handle. They are also available in many different cross-sections and sizes as well as sometimes having curved blades.

The possible range of carving tools is infinite, but towards the end of the nineteenth century a degree of standardisation was introduced together with a numerical system for identification based on the curvature of the cross-section and the bend of the blade but not the width of the tool. In this system nos. 1 to 11 are all straight-bladed tools with cross-sections ranging from flat (no. 1) through a series of gradually deepening curves up to no. 9 which is semicircular. Nos. 10 and 11 are semicircular with extended sides to give deeper cuts. No. 12 corresponds to no. 3. in cross-section but has a curved blade; no. 24 is the same but 'front bent' like a spoon and 33 is the same again but 'back bent' for cutting over rounded forms. Between 39 and 46 the tools are V-shaped and after that the numbers refer to the various specialised forms shown in the Table of Woodcarving Gouges overleaf. Each of these numbered tools may be available in as many as seventeen or eighteen different widths up to two inches, so that a full description of a particular tool must give the width as well as the number and possibly also the name—'No. 12, $\frac{3}{4}$ inch,* curved' or 'No. 24, $\frac{1}{2}$ inch, front bent'.

If the sixty-six shapes noted on the Table were all available in eighteen different widths the carver would be faced with a choice of nearly twelve hundred tools. However, such a range is quite unnecessary; a professional carver may possess seventy or eighty tools of which he uses constantly about a dozen. As we shall see later, no more than half a dozen are necessary for carving bowls of many shapes and sizes, but duplicates of some of the basic shapes are often useful as the children or their friends are always wanting to work at the same time!

Handles may be made from ash, beech, mahogany, rosewood, lignum vitae, box or other hardwoods and will be found in many different shapes. Tapered octagonal or hexagonal forms have been popular and as they are less likely to roll off the bench (potentially one of the greatest dangers in the craft as a heavy gouge generally falls blade downwards) have a distinct advantage over round ones, but it is sometimes pointed out that a variety of shapes and colours gives each tool a personality of its own and makes it easy to find. The larger tools which are more likely to be used with a mallet should have brass ferrules on the handles to prevent the blades from splitting them.

*One inch = 25.4 mm.

	Straight	Curved Salmon Bend	Front Bent Spoon bit	Back Bent Spoon Bit	Fishtail Spade Long Spade Allongee	Sections
CHISELS Corner, Skew or entering (right or left)	1 2		21 22 23		61 62	
GOUGES (semi-circular)	3 4 5 6 7 8 9	12 13 14 15 16 17 18	24 25 26 27 28 29 30	33 34 35 36 37 38	63 64 65 66 67 68 69	
Fluters	10	19	31		70	
Veiners	11	20	32		71	
Parting 60° 45° 90°	39 41 45	40 42 46	43 44			
	47					
	48					
Macaroni	49	50				
Flutaroni	51		52			
Backaroni						

80 Side chisel   81 Foot Chisel   82 Dog leg

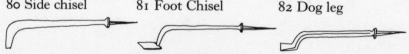

N.B.   Some manufacturers prefix the numbers shown above with two more digits to identify their own products.

MALLETS

The mallet acts as an extension of the arm muscles and in choosing a took of this kind it should be borne in mind that there is a distinct relationship between the work it will be called upon to do and its weight. A light mallet used with a large gouge for heavy roughing out work, or 'bosting in', requires forceful driving from the forearm whereas a heavier mallet, more suited to the scale of the work, will achieve the same result without the use of the forearm muscles at all. This is a very important point; if the mallet is too light the muscles are tensed in bringing it down and receive a shock at each impact which eventually damages the connecting tissues between them and the bones. The result of such damage is painful* and when it has occurred the affected arm may be useless for carving, carrying or any other activity for weeks or even months. This happened to me soon after I became engrossed in woodcarving. Since then I have learned to control the feverishness of my desire to get on, to lunge gently at the work rather to smash at it, and consequently to progress a great deal faster. It is an old story usually illustrated by the digging performance of amateur or professional gardeners, but, in the crafts, there is another side to it, perhaps most evident in the throwing of pots on a wheel. Nothing can be achieved in this business until the thrower's finger and hand muscles are relaxed enough to feel the reactions of the clay and the evolving form. Yet the beginner can never relax so that a vicious circle of insensitivity is set up which sometimes lasts a lifetime! In woodcarving there is not, of course, the immediacy of throwing; the work slowly appears out of the block instead of rushing up in our hands, but its form still has to be felt and the gouge guided to shape what we want. Can this be achieved in a state of physical tension?

*A similar situation sometimes arises from the incorrect use of tennis rackets and the condition has become known as 'tennis elbow'. Every tool used with a hitting action should be heavy enough to do the work expected from it with its own mass—a rule which readily extends to saws, planes, drills, rakes, sickles, scissors and so many other tools.

A skilled letter cutter uses a mallet weighing about $1\frac{1}{2}$ lbs* on soft
stones. Such a weight is perfectly adequate for most of the finishing
work in woodcarving using gouges up to an inch in width against the
ordinary range of hardwoods. A lighter mallet, around $1\frac{1}{4}$ lbs, is useful
for similar work in softer woods or for finer cutting on hardwoods. For
clearing large volumes of material using deep gouges of around one
inch—no. 9 or 10 for example—a mallet weighting 2 lbs is minimal,
$2\frac{1}{2}$ lbs would allow the work to proceed faster. The $1\frac{1}{2}$ or 2 inch gouges
require a mallet of about 3 lbs in weight if any advantage in speed of
clearing is to be gained from using them.

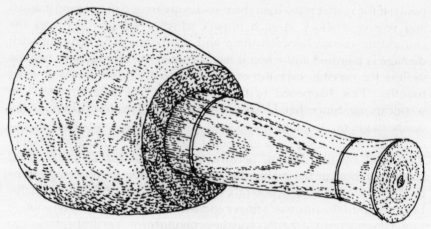

Woodcarver's mallet.

It follows then that for a mallet to be of a convenient size as well as
weight it must be made from a fairly dense wood. Lignum vitae is the
current favourite but other woods have been employed for mallets and
beech is used for lighter ones. Small heavy mallets can sometimes be
obtained made from lead alloys or malleable iron, but the harder metals
used for ordinary hammers, or the general purpose 4 lb 'lump' or 'mash
hammers' commonly available in tool shops, are not suitable for carving
in any material as they do not absorb shock.

*1 lb = .4536 kg (approximately 450 g); 1 in = 25.4 mm.

1. The 'great oval dish' described in Chapter One.

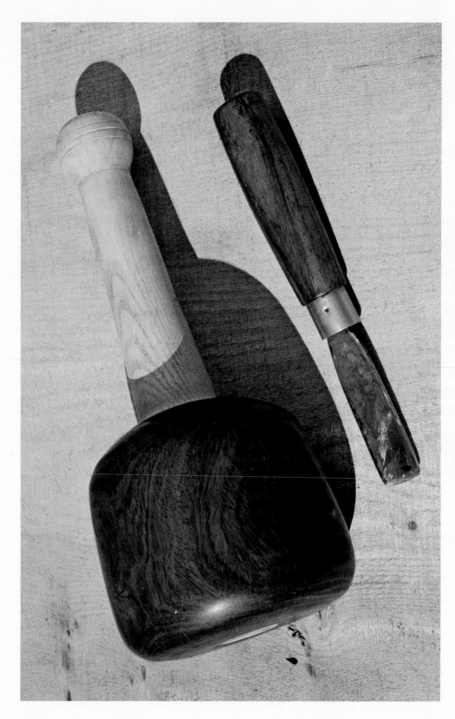

2. Mallet turned from a discarded 'wood' by Geoffrey Hawkins and handmade gouge (see pages 62 to 64). The mallet, with a length of 10″ and weight of 2 lbs 6 ozs (1077 g), is superbly balanced for heavy work.

The round, slightly conical form of the carver's mallet does not appear to have changed for thousands of years. They are usually listed in tool merchants' catalogues by diameter of head and it will be found that in lignum vitae a 5 inch one weighs about 3 lbs, a 4 inch one about 2 lbs and a 3 inch one 1 lb. In beech a 4 inch mallet weighs only 1 lb or so.

PLANES

The earliest plane was simply a wide chisel held firmly in a block to give some control over the depth of its cut and the tool existed in this crude form almost without alteration for many centuries. Whether the block is of metal or wood—and many Roman planes were iron—makes little difference, for the refinements which make the modern steel plane such a delight to use by comparison with its predecessors are not dependent upon the body; they are the result of improvements in the blade metal, its thinner section, the angle of its seating, the ease of adjustment and in the provision of a 'cap iron'.

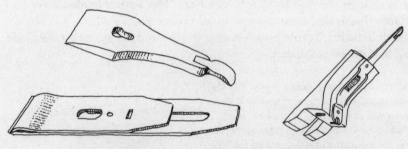

The important parts of a modern plane: a) lever cap; b) cap iron in position on the cutting iron; c) the frog.

The purpose of the cap iron is to break the grain of the shaving and curl it up in the throat of the plane so that the tendency for the cut to run ahead of the blade edge, as though a wedge were being driven along just under the surface, is eliminated. The position of the cap iron is adjustable; when it is set within a fraction of an inch of the cutting edge the curling action commences immediately, but if it is set back by as much as $\frac{1}{32}$ inch the curling action is delayed so that the wedge effect is allowed to come into play a little beforehand.

In conjunction with adjustments of the cap iron the blade itself can be made to project to a greater or lesser amount beyond the sole and it can be set forwards or backwards in the mouth. A wide mouth in front of the blade, deep projection of the blade and setting back the cap iron makes for rapid work and a rough finish on softwoods and tough work—possibly too tough—on hardwoods. The finest settings at each of these three points ensures smooth operation and paper thin slices.

In modern bench planes adjustment of the cap iron is made by a locking screw when both irons are out of the plane; projection of the cutting edge is controlled by a large milled nut inside the loop of the handle and setting of the position of the blade within the mouth is controlled by two screws, one locking and one adjusting, which fix the seating of the irons (the 'frog') into the chassis of the plane. Two further refinements in modern planes are the provision of a 'lateral adjusting lever' behind the iron which allows quick alterations to be made if the blade is projecting a little unevenly through the mouth, and the 'lever cap' which clamps the two irons into position. The spring loaded lever cap replaces the wedge arrangement in all earlier planes which was always difficult to fix firmly into position after the desired projection of the blade itself had been established.

Modern smoothing plane showing the positions of adjusting screws, lock nuts and irons. The frog is locked with a vertical screw, but this can be loosened to allow the mouth to be narrowed for fine work.

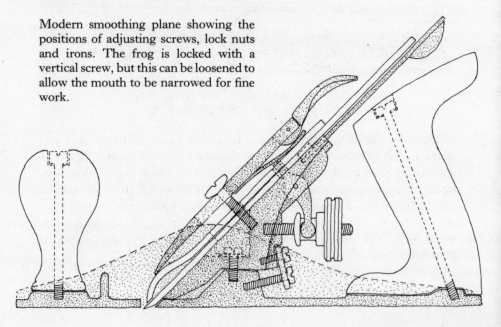

There are, of course, many different kinds of plane. The features so far described are all evident in Jack planes (about 15 inches long and by far the most useful tool for everyday levelling work—literally the 'Jack of All Trades'), the 'try' plane (about 22 inches long), the 'shooting' plane (longer than 22 inches) and the smaller 'smoothing' plane (about 8 inches) which is set very finely for finishing work. A Jack or smoothing plane will be found useful occasionally for removing the rough marks left by chain saws sufficiently to allow the wood to be marked up with fine lines, but for the type of work described in these pages the smaller 'block' plane which can be held in one hand is by far the most useful. This plane was evolved for smoothing the end grain of butcher's blocks for which purpose a low angle of blade (about 20° as against 45° of the smoothing plane) is necessary and a cap iron irrelevant as there is no question of a long shaving coming off the end of the grain.

The cutting bevel of a block plane will be found on the upper surface of the blade whereas on all bench planes fitted with cap irons it has to be located on the lower surface. Because of this the grinding of the bevel in block planes is especially critical and the tool will not operate effectively if the angle is allowed to increase much beyond about 25° through constant sharpening of the tip only. This arrangement is consistent with many single iron planes through history, but it has never been standardised and the point needs watching—a low angled seating always implies that the bevel should be on top, whilst steeper angles of seating—30° or more—suggest the opposite.

Modern steel block plane with screw adjustment for the iron.

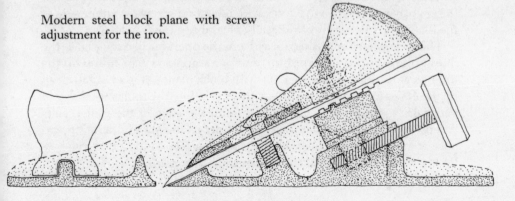

There are a number of shapes and sizes of block planes about, including one with a specially low angled blade ($12\frac{1}{2}°$) and an adjustable mouth (Stanley No. $60\frac{1}{2}$) which is ideal for the varied conditions of grain to be found over the outsides of bowls or around their rims. When purchased new the bodies of steel planes are too angular for the comfort of the hands and it well worth while spending an hour or more with a file and slipstone removing all the corners or sharp edges so that the tool becomes a pleasure to hold.

SPOKESHAVES

A spokeshave is simply a plane adapted to take the place of the primitive draw knife which is still sometimes used for rapidly converting square sawn spokes to round or oval sections and tapering their ends to fit into holes in the hub or rim. Its general usefulness in carpentry work—particularly chairmaking—was quickly recognised and it soon became a standard tool with a number of variants for special purposes. Several patterns are produced for to-day's market and these are as refined in design and operation as the modern steel plane, although the securing lever cap of the plane is replaced by a cap iron held in position with a thumb screw. No separate cap iron is attached to the blade which is, nevertheless, seated bevel downwards.

The two most useful spokeshaves to us are the flat soled version for convex curves—the outside surfaces and rims of bowls—and the round soled version for shaping the inner curvature of rims or concave surfaces. Both are available without screw adjustments to the blades, but the slightly more expensive tools with adjusting screws at either side of the blade are a better buy and really pleasant to use.

The spokeshave is pushed away from the operator like the plane (the draw knife is pulled towards him) and two seatings will be found for the thumbs at the back of the tool. As with block planes, it is a help to clean up the edges of the body casting with a file before the tool is used and in particular to polish very carefully around the edge of the milled sole. Attention to this latter point is well rewarded in ease of operation and once a spokeshave has been brought into perfect condition it removes timber from curved surfaces more quickly than rasps or Surform tools, leaving, at the same time, a pleasing faceted surface.

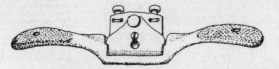

Adjustable spokeshave made from cast 'malleable' iron.

Section of spokeshave showing adjustment mechanism, curved sole and flat sole (dotted).

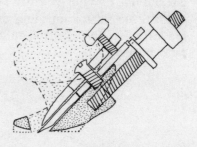

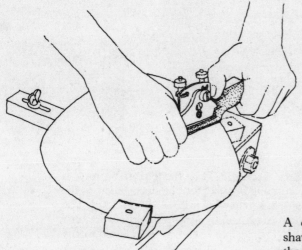

A child using a spokeshave in conjunction with the clamp shown on p. 101.

MINOR TOOLS

A really good bit for a brace—as wide as possible and, preferably, spiralled so that it will not jam in its own shavings in a deep hole—is a great help in starting off bowls and a fine cut file is often a help in tidying up rims or an occasional exterior surface which is too small or irregular in grain to get at with a spokeshave. Rasps followed by bastard, second cut and fine files (all of which need regular cleaning with a wire brush) are very useful for finishing the surfaces of sculptures and the finer grades of sandpaper—160 to 200 mesh—are often necessary for the same purpose.

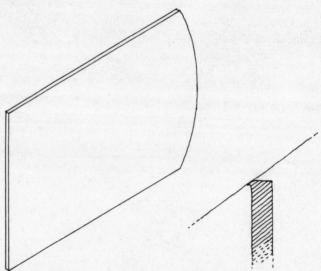

Cabinet maker's scraper. This flexible steel tool is sharpened by rubbing a hard piece of steel—such as the back of a gouge—down the edge to form a burr (right). The edge needs trueing with a file or oilstone before a worn burr can be replaced. The scraper itself can be adapted to any curve by filing.

Occasionally it may be desirable to eradicate completely tool marks inside or outside a bowl, in which case the cabinet maker's scraper, suitably modified in shape with a file, is safer than a piece of broken glass.

Such tools as the 'crooked adze' or 'bottomer' (modified adzes used for rough bowls and chair seats) are difficult to handle and probably best left in the capable hands of specialist craftsmen.

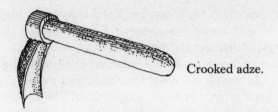

Crooked adze.

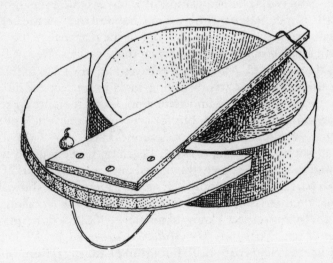

Implement (evolved from a precision engineering tool) for locating the centres of circular forms. The loop of string is stretched across the back to find the centre line across the base.

Chapter Four

SHARPENING

Looking back to the beginning of my woodcarving, I realise now that my earlier experience of working in stone was somewhat of a handicap in that it led me unconsciously to expect the two materials to respond to chisels in much the same way. I was content if small chips flew off the wood as they do off stone and it took me some time to master the art of removing the bulk of surplus timber in huge gougefuls and following this operation by successive degrees of fine paring until the desired form had been achieved. The acquisition of a few woodcarvers' gouges in place of the firmer gouge mentioned in Chapter One was the beginning of a change of approach towards wood, but the real change did not take place until I had also learned to sharpen these gouges effectively.

It was the same with planes, spokeshaves and saws. Up to this time I had not used first class woodworking tools in perfect condition and perhaps this is not an uncommon situation. Good tools are an acquired taste; they can still be bought, but for every good one—new or second hand—there are dozens of nearly useless ones in the run-of-the-mill-do-it-yourself shops of the High Street. Learning to distinguish between the two and to bring the newly purchased ones up to a condition for use is as much part of the development of tactile experience as the making of a bowl or the three dimensional forms Henry Moore is talking about on page 28. In this respect I know of no more evocative description than the chapter on Tools in *The Village Carpenter* by Walter Rose (Cambridge 1937 and 1946; E. P. Publishing Ltd. 1973) from which the following quotation is drawn:

The sound of tools properly used is as a pleasing tune. The craftsman has no need to examine a saw to know if it is sharp, or if it is handled properly. Nor need he look at a plane to know if it functions at its best. The ill-used tool makes a discordant noise which is agony to the trained ear. The sound of the hammer driving the nail, or releasing or securing the wedge of the plane, in each case has its separate and distinctive note. The blow of the mallet on the chisel tells by its sound alone whether or not the user has the confidence of ability. The multitude of sounds of tools at work on wood is a separate language known to the woodworker, and each separate note is recognised with satisfaction or dislike. An unexpected note at once arrests attention; especially the shriek of protest from the saw that has struck an unsuspected nail. This is the horror of horrors to the wood craftsman; it sends a shudder through the whole workshop.

In the absence of any professional guidance about sharpening I evolved methods for myself which, although unconventional, have certainly proved effective and perhaps easier for the novice than those described in woodworkers' manuals. Basically these methods consist of taking the stone to the tool—gouge, chisel or plane blade—instead of the tool to the stone and arranging the two so that it is always possible to see the angle between them. Gouges are propped up on a piece of wood and rotated by the left hand whilst the stone is rubbed against them with the right. Plane or spokeshave blades and chisels are set on their sides in wooden blocks. In all cases (*see overleaf*) I can watch the progress of the work, although to see properly what has been achieved it is necessary to wipe away the oil at intervals and to peer at the edge through a powerful magnifying glass. This latter instrument has taught me as much about sharpening as anything else.

EDGE SHAPES

However, before any tool can be sharpened successfully it is necessary to know something about the shape of edge which will work most effectively. With regard to gouges there is apparently a degree of personal preference about the edge shapes and some variation of requirement according to the hardness of the wood being carved. I learned most from a pair of one inch gouges which were acquired from a

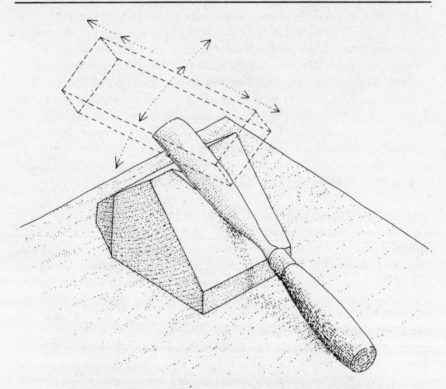

An easy method of sharpening a gouge. The gouge is held with the left hand and rotated until the angle of the stone—which is rubbed vigorously in all directions to minimise wear—is visible. The corner of the block which can be seen under the stone is cut to 25° to give some guide to the angle of sharpening. Oil is applied to the stone or the tip of the gouge. The inside of the gouge is treated in the same way, using the round edge of a slipstone at a shallower angle.

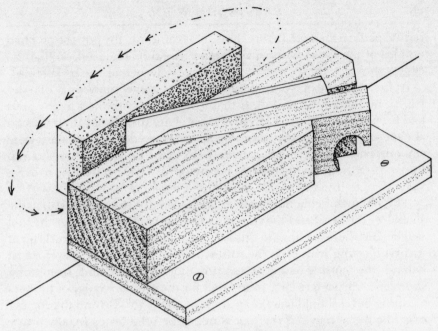

Jigs for sharpening plane irons and chisels, designed by the author (Patents applied for). The correct angles for sharpening the bevels or honing the tips are obtained by using either side of the wedge in the plane iron jig or changing the position of the peg in the one for chisels.

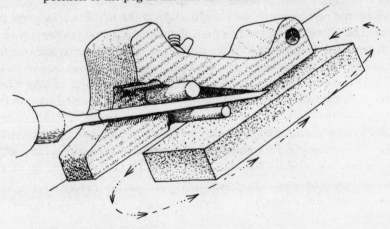

retired pattern maker.* Before these tools came into my possession I had
no idea of the speed with which timber could be removed, so that the
ease with which these two old gouges cut it away took me by surprise.

At first this ease of working was attributed to the 'superiority of older
steels', but later it became clear that it was to do with the way the tools
had been sharpened. As I ran my finger along their backs there was no
abrupt slope of a bevel towards the cutting edge; the blades were
smooth, polished and gently curved right to the tip so that they slid into
the wood without having to force the cut open. I had been trying to drive
steep wedges into the wood—no wonder the work had been heavy!

The obvious deduction from this elementary discovery is that the
shallower the bevel and the smoother the curvature the sharper the tool
will be, but there is a limit to this rule beyond which the edge curls up at
its first meeting with even the softest timber. Some thickness of metal
behind the cutting edge is essential for strength and from long
experience carpenters have found that for the ordinary range of timbers
a cutting bevel should start at an angle of about $30°$. Behind the cutting
edge the metal may—if the tool is not to be used for especially heavy
work like driving mortices into oak frames—be bevelled away at about
$25°$, and, if the tool is to be used for very light work, such as the cleaning
of tenons, these angles can be reduced to $25°$ at the tip backed up by a
main bevel of around $20°$.

These angles assume that the other side of the blade is rubbed
perfectly flat on the stone. Any slight angle at the tip of this face has the
effect of blunting the tool rather than sharpening it, and yet the novice is
often tempted to bevel both faces of a blade in his effort to remove the
rough burr or 'wire edge' that develops as soon as the tip begins to be
tapered down to nothing. This burr can be felt by running a finger along
to the tip of the face opposite to that which was being honed, but with the
first rub of this face against the stone the burr bends the other way.
Under a magnifying glass the burr can be seen quite easily and it can be
removed by drawing the edge across the corner of a piece of scrap wood,
like a schoolboy making the first cut for a notch in the edge of his desk.

*Pattern makers are very skilled craftsmen who make the wooden models from
which moulds are prepared for metal castings. They use either pine or
mahogany.

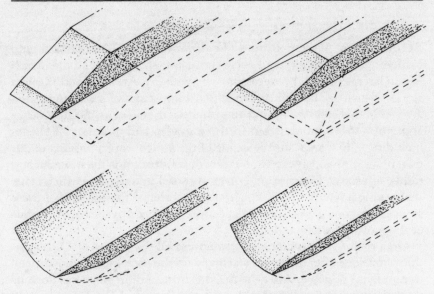

Sharpening angles: a) plane blades or firmer chisels (30°; 25°); b) paring chisels (25°; 20°); c) firmer gouge (30°; 25°); d) woodcarving chisel.

When the burr has gone the edge will be sharp, although it may be marred by slight scratches, caused by the stone, which terminate at the tip like small teeth and it will perform better if it is now polished.

The sharpening of a woodcarver's gouge is different from chisels and plane blades in several respects. First, as we have seen, the tool works best if the various angles of the bevel are run into one another without abrupt changes. Then the bevels are also shallower and longer to give smoother entry into the wood and the shallowness of angle at the tip is compensated by a small bevel—again smoothed out to a gentle curve— on the opposite face of the tool making the aggregate of angles between these two slopes up to about the usual 30°. In hardwoods a tool sharpened in this fashion is admirable, although many carvers have found that the small bevel on the inner face does not work well on softwood. Here the traditional 20/25° bevels of the carpenters' paring chisels applied to one face only seem best.

SHARPENING STONES

According to Walter Rose (*The Village Carpenter*) carvers and carpenters of this century have been using sharpening stones which would have sent their predecessors wild with joy. Arkansas and Washita stones, which are best for the final polishing stages of sharpening, first arrived in this country around 1890 and the excellent artificial stones—India or Carborundum, sold in three grades and a variety of shapes including 'slip stones' for the inside of the gouge—are a product of our own times. Previously craftsmen were dependent upon the irregular and rather soft slates, Charnwood Forest, Ayr or Turkey stones which made sharpening a lengthy process, although, perhaps, the softness of these stones in bygone days is somewhat counterbalanced by the harder metals of the tools of to-day.

On a major resharpening craftsmen use all the grades of Carborundum stone one after the other, starting with the coarsest to remove metal as rapidly as possible. After the finest Carborundum stone has done its work the bevels are polished with a slip of Arkansas or Washita stone and buffed on a leather strop soaked in oil and impregnated with the finest grade of emery powder. A useful emery cloth is also available for this purpose.

It is advisable to keep a set of stones especially for plane blades, as gouges or narrow chisels inevitably work the stones into hollows no matter how rotary the motion with which they are used. Thin oil is employed in conjunction with all these stones to keep the heat down, as well as to remove the particles of metal, and occasionally a stone will need unclogging with a wash of paraffin, turpentine or petrol.

GRINDING

New gouges are supplied with only a roughly ground bevel and the amount of work involved in smoothing this away to a shallow curve, or drastically altering the shape of an older tool, using only the three grades of Carborundum stone, would be phenomenal. Some form of grindstone is essential for this task and if you do not possess one yourself a friendly garage or workshop will usually allow one of theirs to be used for half an hour or so.

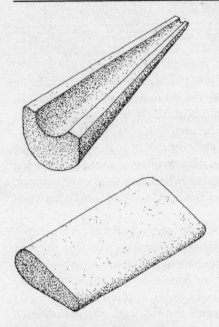

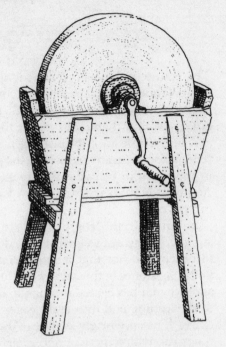

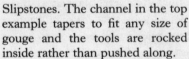

Slipstones. The channel in the top example tapers to fit any size of gouge and the tools are rocked inside rather than pushed along.

Sandstone grinding wheel.

The old sandstone wheels operated by two people—one turning the stone whilst the other holds the tool—are ideal for our purpose as they rotate in a trough of water which keeps the metal cool throughout the operation and the stone itself free from clogging particles. These noble wheels are not very often seen these days as the supply of good stone and labour to dress them has largely dried up, and besides, the electrically driven Carborundum stones which have replaced them allow one person to do the work very much more quickly.

It is, though, easy to ruin a steel tool on an electric grindstone by reversing the heat treatment to which the tool had been subjected during manufacture and it is essential to have a pan of water near the grinder in which to cool the tool down after each stroke against the wheel.

MAKING A GOUGE

The nature of the heat treatment applied to steel tools can usefully be demonstrated by converting an old file into a gouge or chisel. In chemical composition the steel of a file is quite close to that of a gouge, but in physical characteristics the file is very different. It is hard, brittle and impossible to cut or sharpen, although if it is heated to bright redness for about an hour within the coals of an open fire, and then buried in the ashes to cool slowly, the excessive hardness leaves the metal. Another file rubbed across it now leaves a bright surface and a hacksaw can cut it.

So cut down the length of a file to something reasonable for a gouge* and then grind away slowly to the desired form (never allowing the tool to become so hot that it requires quenching), finishing with oil and polishing stones in the usual way. Put the finished tool back into the fire, and, when it has heated through to bright redness, plunge an inch or so of the leading end into tepid water until the violence of the bubbling ceases. The once bright surface of the metal will now be blackened, but a quick rub with a piece of fine emery paper pinned to a stick will revive the brightness. Immediately a light yellow colour will be seen to creep down the bright metal from the uncooled mass of the tool and as more heat spreads back down to the tip the yellow will turn darker, then brown, then dark brown followed by light purple, dark purple and blue. When the dark yellow band has reached the tip plunge the whole tool into tepid water and leave it until all the heat has gone. The gouge has now been rehardened or tempered (but not to the point of brittleness) so that it can be given a final sharpening and polish like any other gouge.†
The hard brittleness of the original file would have returned at this point

*Snapping the file in its brittle state is of course quicker, but very dangerous unless it is wrapped in cloth or newspaper to prevent the two ends—especially the tang—from flying about.

†Alternatively, if a localised heat source is available, such as a gas flame, the tempering of the gouge can be accomplished by heating the leading inch or so to

if the whole tool had been suddenly quenched in *cold water* from the red heat of the final tempering.

The various tempers a tool can be given are explained by the character of the crystal structure of the metal at the heat on quenching, and the nature of the structure is further affected by the chemical composition of the steel. For instance, gouges are made from 'high carbon steel' which is iron alloyed with between 0.65 and 0.9% of carbon: files are made from ultra high carbon steel containing between 0.9 and 1.5% of carbon—slightly more than is in commercial gouges. When the carbon in a steel is lower than 0.25% (mild steel) the product is useful only for ships' plates, girders or reinforcing rods, and below 0.1% it is useful only for tinplating, conduit pipes etc.

Carbon alloys with iron during the smelting process from which the first product is 'pig' or 'cast' iron, a particularly brittle and unworkable material containing anything up to 4 or 5% of this non-metallic element. To turn cast iron into steel this high carbon content has to be reduced to the levels indicated above by such means as blowing oxygen through the iron whilst it is still molten, and the range of physical properties of the finished product is controlled, not only by manipulation of the carbon content, but also by the addition of other metals. For instance, we hear of 'tungsten steel' which does not require tempering; 'cobalt steel' which can retain a cutting edge at high temperatures; 'manganese steel' which is non-magnetic and 'silicon/manganese steel' which is acid resistant and tough enough to serve as armour plate.

The various colours travelling down the bright polished surface of steel during tempering will be familiar to older potters as the colours of the long range of iron oxides which used to be sold by the merchants in Stoke-on-Trent. As the bright metal is reheated from the unquenched part of the tool these oxides form on the surface, grading from one to the other as the heat increases. The tempers are as follows, and, although this method of tempering may seem rough and ready, it has sufficed for

---

redness, quenching it and polishing it, and then reheating gently about one inch behind the tip until the darker yellow or straw colour is showing there. This method leaves the handle end of the tool less brittle which is an advantage in heavy work.

the village blacksmith or toolmaker for centuries. It will be noticed that the lowest heat for the final tempering produces the hardest tool, and, as the electric grindstone yields dark purple or blue immediately, in the hands of a careless operator, the hardness of the cutting edge is removed.

The tempering of steels

Increasing heat—
decreasing hardness

light yellow—metal turning tools
   yellow—engineer's machine tools
dark yellow—metal dies and punches; gouges
  (straw)
   brown—engineers' taps and cold chisels
dark brown—drills, axes, wood chisels and plane irons.
light purple—saws and knives
dark purple—large saws and screwdrivers
  dark blue—springs

The 'wrought iron' mentioned on page 38 was manufactured by softening the ore, rather than melting it, whilst the carbon of the fuel—generally charcoal—took away the oxide element. The resulting softened spongy mass or bloom was then beaten with heavy hammers or 'wrought', with continual reheating, to form it into a cohesive metal billet. During the hammering some of the slag from the rocky part of the ore flew out as flakes of shale, but some remained in the metal drawn out into fibres. This fibrous slag content of wrought iron played a very important part in the properties of the final material making it rustless, easy to weld and exceptionally malleable at comparatively low temperatures. A low carbon content can be induced back into the surface of wrought iron by continually heating it in a bed of charcoal, but the result is not as good a tool metal as a modern steel derived from molten iron from which the slag has been separated by the difference of density of liquid rock and liquid metal.

There is, though, another factor in favour of wrought iron and this is the strength imparted to the metal by beating, which is in direct contrast to cast iron where the metal crystals lie in disorderly formation just as they cooled. This contrast affects a gouge ground out of a file rather than beaten out and it would be unwise therefore to subject such a cast tool to heavy blows or to the wrenching action of a wood turning lathe.

HOLLOW GRINDING

The small diameter of modern electric grindstones leaves pronounced hollow bevels when the edges of tools are passed across them and this concave shape has become popular for plane blades, chisels, knives and other tools. While it is true that hollow ground bevels of this kind are better than convex ones formed by incorrect sharpening, I find that they crumble against hard woods. A flat bevel at the correct angle behind the cutting edge seems preferable, although the hollow bevel is satisfactory on softwoods or for such instruments as carving knives, razors etc. A compromise solution for blades which are already poorly shaped is to grind the bevel to a hollow and then follow immediately by sharpening the tip at 25° and 30° with flat Carborundum stones.

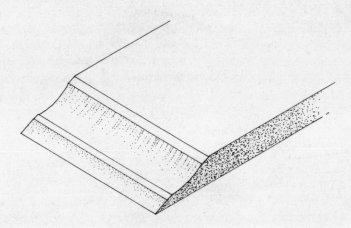

Hollow grinding.

SHARPENING SAWS

The sharpening of saws is an entirely different undertaking and although it used to be possible to send them away for expert treatment the quality of this service has generally declined through the introduction of machines. There are also many saws about with hardened teeth, Teflon coatings or replaceable blades, which cannot be resharpened, so that when their efficiency begins to decline nothing can be done to them. Where a great deal of sawing is to be done it seems therefore economical to acquire tools of the older type and to learn to resharpen them for oneself. The adjustable Eclipse saw setting and sharpening tools are a help to the novice and a good magnifying glass on a stand is a blessing for working on fine teeth.

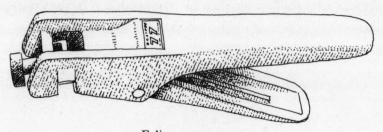

Eclipse saw setter.

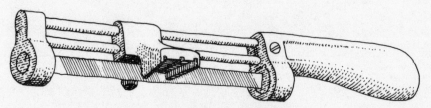

Eclipse saw sharpener.

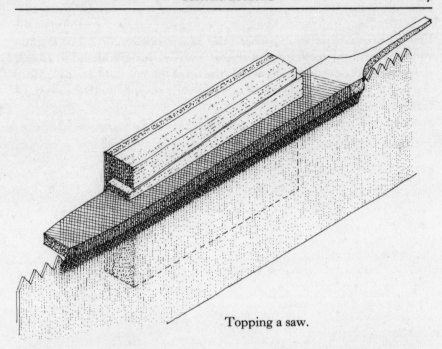

Topping a saw.

The process is carried out in four stages. First the tops of the teeth are filed level ('topping') with a file set in a block of wood. The teeth are then shaped evenly to the angles noted on pages 33 to 36 by filing across the saw at right angles using the correct size of file. After 'shaping' the teeth are 'set' to give a cut no more than half as wide again as the saw, and, finally, the teeth are sharpened by passing the file between them again, this time at an angle instead of at right angles. The precise angle of sharpening varies again according to the purpose of the saw, but the Eclipse tool gives an average which is satisfactory for most handsaws. The larger teeth of two-handled saws can be sharpened quite easily without a guide.

In all these processes the 'clamp base' described on page 101 can be adapted as a saw vice, or a short length of the blade can be fixed in an ordinary vice between boards which allow only about half an inch of the blade to project above them.

Walter Rose in *The Village Carpenter* again reveals something of the fine art of saw sharpening where the saw is not levelled, but slightly rounded, and the teeth are not shaped evenly, but graduated to ensure that most of the cutting is done after the tip of the saw has been eased into the wood. Perhaps one day we shall be equally responsive to the needs of timber and tools!

Chapter Five

TREES

When I first set out hoping to acquire some timber suitable for carving from the massive bulk of a freshly felled elm I was defeated. As I clambered over its gigantic trunk and shattered branches clutching a tiny log saw it was obvious that there was nothing I could do and I turned away, awed by the majesty of this thing spread out across the furrows of a ploughed field, saddened by the callousness with which it had been mown down and humbled by its strength. The experience was profoundly disturbing. Had I to become dependent upon those ruthless gangs of log merchants, who, in recent years, have been raping the countryside with chain saws, the farmers who are still rooting out their hedgerows, or to join the 'half-way craftsmen' of all kinds who obtain their materials from suppliers, neither knowing nor caring where they have come from or what they were like in their raw states?

While I was turning over these problems in my mind there was, of course, no alternative to visiting local saw mills where one could watch the great trunks like those I had clambered over being swung about and reduced to planks with consummate ease and fearsome noise, or to beg for offcuts from the various workshops in the neighbouring towns and villages. The supply from these sources was plentiful for my small requirements and it was quite easy to acquire, at nominal prices, adequate pieces of elm, ash, sycamore and lime.

But, everywhere I met sadness and anxiety. Wood is scarce, expecially the traditional English hardwoods, and the timber world clearly in disarray. If my requests had been for even modest quantities of dry seasoned material of any quality I should have been sent from yard to yard and returned home empty in hand or pocket. We are paying the price for years of neglect and mechanisation on the farms and only in books read nostalgically of the days of the Village Carpenter, when the

man called in to repair a mill or barn roof could walk around with the
farmer to select, from dozens in his hedgerows, just the tree to provide
what was needed.

REPLENISHMENT

It is worth pausing for a moment to remind ourselves how essential trees
are on farms and the seriousness of the present crisis for the chemistry of
the soil, as well as for those dependent upon trees for their livelihoods as
carpenters, log merchants or even nut collectors.

The roots of mature trees extend down into the soil perhaps forty
feet*—far deeper than any other plants—and from this great depth
bring up into the crown dissolved mineral salts which were long ago
washed out of the fertile top soil. These reclaimed salts are concentrated
for the most part in the leaves and fruits and the bulk of the moisture in
which they were dissolved is exhaled back into the atmosphere, through
pores in the leaves, at the rate of two or three hundred gallons a day at the
height of the growing season. Alongside this reclamation process of
moisture and plant nutrients from the depth of the subsoil, the leaves
also extract carbon dioxide from the atmosphere (the chief pollutant
from exhaust pipes and chimneys) for conversion into the wood itself,
and in exchange give off oxygen. At the end of the season the bulk of the
reclaimed mineral salts are returned to the top soil, together with a
considerable amount of humus, which is essential for good soil
structure, through the shedding of the leaves and fruits. In physical terms,
trees also break the speed of winds across a landscape and provide
accommodation for countless birds that live off insects and pests.

In parts of the south and east of Britain (and many other parts of the
world) the tree population has been reduced to the point at which it has
become difficult to sustain agriculture without virtually complete
dependence upon chemical fertilizers and insecticides, giving no latitude
for the occasional prolonged dry spell or breaks for gale force winds
which may follow them. While the oil supplies upon which so many
'agro-chemicals' are based were still plentiful such dependence was
thought to be economical, labour saving (although of labour there is a

*About 12 metres.

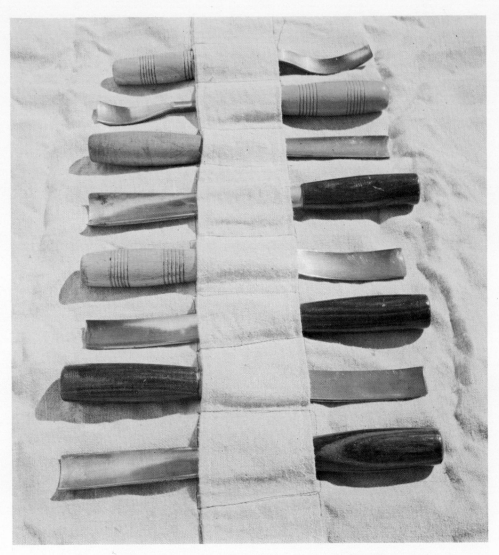

3. The author's favourite gouges for bowlmaking.
From the front – no. 7, 1″; no. 13, 1″; no. 16, ¾″; no. 15,
1″; no. 8, 1¼″; no. 6, 1″; no. 27, 1″; no. 16, ¾″.

4. Three similar bowls in different stages showing at the simplest level the evolution of the three-dimensional qualities of disappearing surfaces and space underneath. See page 27.

permanent supply) and worth the risk of top soil erosion, but the coincidence of tree diseases, the great Drought of 1976 and the decline of oil supplies has revealed some of the potential dangers of this policy.

The same farmer who could select from any number of trees from his hedgerows for the repair of his mill or barn carried around every autumn a pocketful of acorns, chestnuts, conkers, beech masts and other seeds ready to push into the soil wherever there was a gap or the need for more cattle shelter. His grandfather had done the same for his benefit and he was thinking of his grandson in the way the good Lord intended.

Here then is where we must start ourselves. Before we have done more than try out our tools on some odd scraps of secondhand timber we are duty bound to investigate what each of us can do now about replacing the timber we shall use in future years. There is nothing at all to prevent us planting seeds by the hundred and if only one survives to maturity the exercise will have have been worthwhile!

Temporarily the hedgerow tree may be out of favour, but if one examines a landscape carefully there are many corners, wayside strips, verges and unused patches of land where a young seedling might struggle through to a size where it becomes recognisable. The chances are then that, as consciousness of the desperate urgency of the need to remedy the ravages of the past decades increases year by year, some at least of your seedlings will be spotted and encouraged to grow on to maturity.

It will be found too that there is a growing willingness among landowners to allow the planting of young trees in agreed places. This is, of course a surer way than the sowing of random seeds and something has already been done on estates affected by elm disease. But this work is expensive for a sapling of this kind requires staking to prevent its insecure roots from being kept loose by the buffeting of wind and often a stout cage to pretect it from cattle. The corners of fields are popular sites because they are inaccessible to modern agricultural machinery. Parks, schools, college sites and the environs of factories offer much scope and most local authorities now have staff who will give advice about where trees can be purchased locally and specific varieties which are suitable for the region. They may also offer saplings free to those who are willing to care for them and during the winter months one or two-year-old trees can be moved from sites where they are unlikely to grow to maturity, perhaps because they are too near to the parent tree, to places where they will have a better chance of survival.

The pleasure of tree planting is exceptional in that it is enhanced year by year: only when we have partaken of it can a felling be ordered or witnessed without, I suspect, deep down there being a feeling of guilt, even though it may have been imperative that the tree in question was felled at that moment. Once down our next responsibility is to make sure that all the timber is used to the best advantage and this is a task that should begin straight away.

UTILISATION

The greater bulk of the twig and shattered branch structure is of course only suitable for firewood or pea sticks, but some of the fatter lengths are usable for fencing posts which are in continual demand. A very few of the major branches may be straight enough for a timber merchant to bother with, but, by and large, these people are interested only in the 'stick' or trunk which they may, if it is very large, cut into two or three lengths on the spot. Various projecting bosses and branch stubs will be removed at the same time so that the heavy lengths of trunk can be seated securely on a lorry.

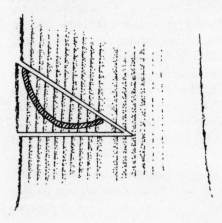

Bowl carved from the wedge cut out of a tree during felling.

It was of course one of these bosses which started me woodcarving and in scrubbing around the sites of fellings I have found others which have been equally usable. A true burr—a boss or swelling caused by the growth of innumerable small branches which have never been able to mature before being snapped off—may in fact yield some very decorative timber, made up entirely of small knots, that will be treasured by veneer cutters, carvers or wood turners, although it is useless for structural work. One may also find large chunks of timber in the wedges cut from the base of the trunk at the commencement of felling and, although the direction of the grain in these pieces may be a little awkward, they come from the best part of the tree where the grain is straightest and most compact. A wedge removed from a very large trunk, and reaching to just beyond the centre of the tree yielded for me a bowl 18 inches in diameter and 6 inches deep.*

SEASONING

During the years when the elm disease was prolific trees were being felled at the height of the growing season and their trunks left around in the fields for months before removal to the sawing mill. This is a bad practice as timber at this season contains the maximum amount of moisture which is able to dry off very quickly from the freshly cut ends, resulting in the rapid development of cracks. Ideally trees should be felled in midwinter when the timber contains the least moisture and the drying conditions are slowest. The trunks should then be removed to the mill and immediately sawn through into planks of the required thickness ready for seasoning.

The mill owner knows of course the dimensions of wood which are in most demand and is in a position to plan his cutting schedule with the

---

*The subsequent history of this bowl is interesting. After it had dried and been oiled for the first time it was accidentally left full of water. After a while a large crack sprang open at the side near the centre of the tree, but within a week or so after the incident the crack closed sufficiently to tempt me to squeeze in some Evostick woodworking glue. The bowl was then resanded and oiled about half a dozen times and put into regular use for bread making without any further trouble. The crack is now barely visible.

best use of the timber in mind. Very often with hardwoods it is a matter
of sawing the trunk through and through (T + T) in slices of two to three
inches* in thickness. The planks ('boards' are under two inches thick)
are then resassembled for seasoning in the order in which they were cut
with spacing sticks ('skids' or 'stickers') between them, making a 'boule'
in an open-sided shed which keeps off direct sun, or rain or snow.

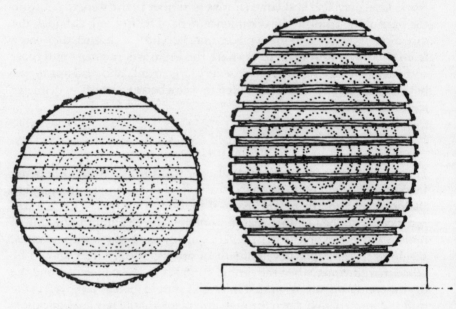

Log sawn 'T + T'.   A boule.

The arrangement of the spacing sticks is done with great care to even
out the drying of the timber as well as the weight of distribution within
the boule. When hardwoods are being stacked in winter the sticks
should be about one inch thick and between two and four feet* apart (two
feet for oak and beech, more for others) for planks two inches or more in

*1 in = 25.4 mm. 1 ft = 304.8 mm (approximately $\frac{3}{10}$ metre).

thickness. In summer, when the atmosphere is dryer, the rate of drying of the timber can be reduced by using half-inch sticks at the same intervals although timber stacked in winter with one inch sticks has generally settled down sufficiently by the summer for it to be unnecessary to reduce the spacing between the boards. Great care is taken to ensure that the sticks are in true vertical alignment, otherwise the weight of the timber is unevenly supported and the planks are warped.

When the boule has been assembled the ends of the planks should be painted with bituminous paint to prevent rapid drying from the end grain, for drying is always accompanied by shrinkage and possibly splitting.

The amount of moisture that newly sawn timber has to lose before it is fit for use in constructional work is considerable—sometimes over one third of its weight (see Table 2, page 94)—and the time taken for this process may be several years. In the hardwood trade a year is allowed for every inch of thickness of the planks if the drying is to take place in the open air and it is not surprising therefore that kilns have been introduced to hasten the turnover of stock in large manufacturing organisations.

Kiln drying is looked upon with suspicion by craftsmen, but when it is properly conducted it reduces the risk of staining and fungus attack in the centres of planks in large boules, where air and light may not penetrate sufficiently, and produces timber more suitable for use inside modern centrally heated buildings. Too rapid kiln drying does, however, harden the outer skin so that the moisture in the centre of the planks has difficulty in escaping and there is always the possibility of drying too much so that the timber has to reabsorb moisture at the surface when the process is over.

The end product of kilning should be no dryer than the atmosphere, which implies that the timber will still contain between 10% and 15% of moisture. Many of the objections to wood dried in this way are caused not by the process itself, but as a result of storing carefully kilned timber in the sodden interiors of buildings under construction or exposed to rain on the site. Storage is in fact the final stage of the seasoning process during which the moisture content evens out with the atmosphere and it is the responsibility of the user to see that this is done properly rather than the supplier.

IN PRAISE OF GREENWOOD

In the fine cabinet, joinery and instrument making worlds, where accuracy of measurement and the fitting of joints are of primary importance, seasoning assumes the propensities of art and is spoken of in mystical terms. Unseasoned timber is 'The Untouchable' and to set good tools to wood from which the sap oozes at each stroke, as I had done at the start of my woodcarving, would indicate a level of insensitivity and ignorance too far outside the credibility of a craftsman for even momentary discussion. Yet my first bowl did not crack and, as I have mentioned, the wood became harder as it dried until it became in parts like iron.

For my next attempts I was determined to do the work 'properly' and to accept the hardness of seasoned wood as an inevitable part of the work of a carver. The products were therefore few and the work itself sometimes more punishing than pleasurable. Slowly though I began to question the need for this self-inflicted agony and to reason with myself that provided a bowl is carved fairly rapidly from soft wet wood it can surely dry out afterwards? It might even be in a better shape to do so than a one inch board because of the ease with which the air would have access to every part of the wood? This did indeed prove to be the case and later I learned that, far from being insensitive or contrary, this is accepted practice in, for instance, the wood turning trade where bowls are turned thickly in the green condition and returned later after the warping caused by uneven shrinkage has settled down.

Warping is due to the wood shrinking more across the grain towards the outer edge of a tree than in the centre and hardly at all down the grain. This happens because the grain consists of long hollow fibres separated from one another by a water layer more evident in the outer sapwood than in the inner heart. The fibres also contain water filled storage cells, which dry out first without affecting the measurements of the wood, but when these cells are empty the surrounding water begins to dry off too, drawing the fibres closer together and causing shrinkage. The unevenness of this shrinkage is often noticeable in planks cut through and through, where the surface nearest the outside of the tree shrinks more than that nearer the centre.

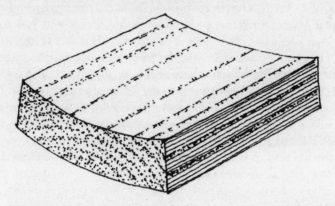

Warping resulting from the increase of shrinkage nearer the outside of the tree.

With regard to bowls, the distortion arising from uneven drying seems to imply that the base should be situated towards the outer edge of the tree with the rim towards the centre and this would allow also the maximum utilisation of the semi-circular cross-section of a half log. However, the extra shrinkage of the base in this position appears sometimes to cause cracks at the rim so that for the moment I work—wastefully—the opposite way. Whether or not a rule can be made on this issue is difficult to judge as several other factors also have a part to play in the avoidance of cracks.

The cross-section of bowls in relation to annual rings; a) maximum utilisation of a half log—base to the outside; b) base to the centre—less cracking.

Green timber stores well under cover in the shady part of a garden. It should be raised from the ground and separated by stickers otherwise moulds and stains develop quite rapidly. When a piece is brought inside for use, the work should be pressed ahead as speedily as possible and always left covered over with a sack or old coat. If it seems likely that no work will be done for several days, the piece should be tucked well away in the dark under the bench where finished objects are also kept until they feel dry enough to bring out into the house. Sunlight is particularly dangerous, but if the wood is very wet it is possible to work in the sun for short spells so long as the work proceeds quickly and the piece is frequently turned round. Shade is preferable. Sculptures in which the wood is thicker and possibly uneven in section can also be carved in wet wood provided still greater care is taken in slowing the drying and the finished piece is not exposed to direct heat or the really warm atmosphere of a living room for a year or so.

The first time I encountered serious warping in a bowl carved from green timber it was disconcerting, but, when one is aware of the amount that is likely to occur, compensation can be made in the preliminary decisions about the form. In general, strong simple forms do not suffer overmuch; there is no more virtue in a truly circular rim than one that has assumed a slight oval with a rhythmical wave line and in accepting such changes as inevitabilities of the method the craftsman's approach can gain in directness. When the warping has finished—and it will be more evident at the start than when all the movement has been completed—the lower part of the form may need slight adjustment and the bottom will certainly need flattening again with a plane.

OBTAINING TIMBER FOR ONESELF

Discovering the virtue of carving in green timber caused me to look afresh at newly felled trees. With a chain saw it would obviously be possible to cut short cylindrical lengths off either the trunk or the larger branches and then to saw down the grain to release suitable blocks for carving. However these noisy and dangerous appliances, which in insensitive hands have been allowed to do untold damage to the countryside, seem alien to a peaceful craft like carving and I settled for the traditional two-handled tree saw (£2 secondhand) with wedges and a

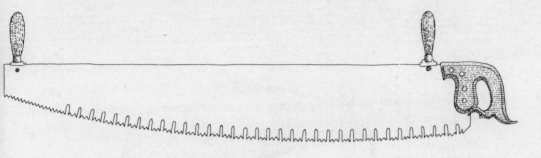

Two handled tree saw.

sledge hammer for splitting down the grain. These tools are a delight
and the business of setting out to acquire blocks for carving has become
an adventure commensurate with the contemplative nature of the work
as a whole.

Before a drum is sawn off a felled 'stick' the cross-sections of the
blocks which could be obtained from it need to be marked out on the end
grain. The measurements of these blocks then provide an indication of
the length which should be sawn off with the first cut. Then wedges are
tapped in lightly all along the ruled lines to start the splitting and finally
the sledge hammer is brought into play against evenly spaced wedges on
each line. If the grain is straight—and of course this fact will be observed
before any energy is expended in sawing off the drum—the splitting is
generally easy and accurate.

My first experience of procuring timber in this way was a salutary
lesson in sheer wastefulness and is recorded here as a warning. From a
pile of trunks I had selected one which was in a convenient position for
myself and some of the younger members of my family to try out the
newly-purchased two-handled saw. The trunk was about thirteen
inches* in diameter and it appeared at a quick glance that if we cut away
the snapped off end for firewood a second cut would release a drum of
prime straight grained timber. This second cut was made about fourteen

*1 in = 2.54 cm.

Splitting a log with a sledge hammer and wedges. Drums of
timber such as this are often cut for logs and provided
they have reasonable depth can yield some usable pieces
for carving as shown by the dotted lines. One segment is
shown sawn and marked out for a bowl. The small lump
hammer is useful for starting the wedges.

inches up the trunk and when it was nearly through the drum fell to the ground with a resounding thump. As it was too heavy to carry far the sledge hammer and wedges were brought to the spot and lines were hastily drawn ready for tapping in. Only when the first lines had been drawn did we notice three radiating cracks (heart shakes) in the centre of the drum so that fresh lines had to be drawn on either side of the centre. The maximum section of blocks that the drum would yield outside the cracks was two pieces 8″ × 4″ in section from which it was possible to make two bowls 8 inches in diameter and 3½ inches deep. As these weighed just ½ lb* each when dry no more than about 1% of the timber had been utilised!†

When freshly felled trees are obtained, for which one has not immediate use, the trunks should be sawn into reasonable lengths, split across the centre—leaving the bark in place—and stacked in a shady place outside after the ends have been dipped in hot wax or painted with bituminous paint. If the trunks are thick it is advisable to split them into quarters before stacking otherwise heart shakes are likely to spread up into the timber as it dries.

CONVERSION

The assessment of suitable places for splitting a log raises the whole question of the 'conversion' of timber in the round to sections suitable for various uses. As we have seen most timber is sawn through and through into planks which can then, after seasoning, be resawn into various widths, leaving only the 'wavy edges' or any seriously cracked or knotted pieces for scrap. This is generally regarded as the most economical method of converting timber for constructional work, although it takes no account of the grain and, in the case of hardwoods, reveals least of their personality.

*1 lb = 453.6 (approximately 450 g).

†Perhaps all was not lost. Every scrap of sawdust from my workshop is spread on the vegetable garden; plane shavings are used on the compost heap or for fire lighting; chippings and offcuts are used as fuel and the ash is either returned again to the garden or used in pottery glazes.

The personality of a timber shows most clearly when a plank is obtained from a radial position in the log. This is because such cuts reveal not only the annual rings but also the 'medullary rays' which radiate from the centre of a tree storing surplus starch (resin in softwoods) for use in the winter period when the supply of fresh sugars from the leaves has stopped. In oak sawn radially the medullary rays are exceptionally evident, but they do not appear when the wood is sawn through and through on any boards apart from those cut through the centre of the log.

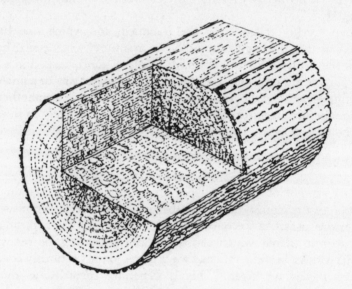

Revealing the medullary rays by direction of cutting.

Attempts to obtain the maximum figuring of annual rings and medullary rays on all the boards cut from one log are wasteful as the diagram at the top of the next page shows, but where the demand justifies it a compromise can be made whereby small figuring is obtained on some of the boards with full figuring on others.

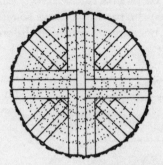 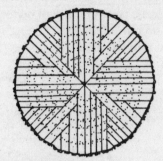

Cutting planks to show figuring.

Apart from the desire to obtain the best appearance in the planks, there is the need to avoid the pith in the very centre of the tree—the original sapling, long since dead—and the heart shakes that so often radiate from it. In some species the outer sapwood is also useless and has to be cut off together with the wavy edge.

Sapwood is, in a sense, living wood in the process of formation and is often both lighter in colour and more prone to insect attack than the 'heartwood' which is the best part of the log. Where the object is to obtain a variety of planks, including some from the strongest part of the wood which might be suitable for flooring, a tree may be sawn as in the diagram below.

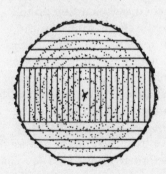

Cutting boards and planks.

Thick timbers suitable for carving or beams can only be obtained from large trees and it will be found that the medullary rays sometimes show on part of an object being carved because at that point the surface lies on a radial plane.

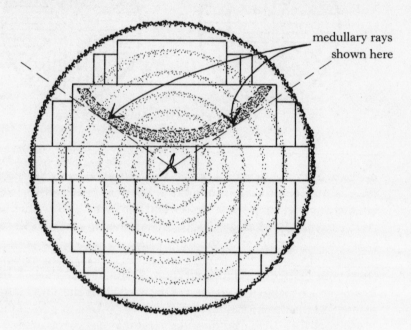

Cutting a log for carving or beams.

The emphasis behind all these traditional schemes for cutting up the trunks and major branches of trees is of course the elimination of waste, although some is impossible to avoid. For instance, the saw itself removes a kerf almost $\frac{1}{4}$ inch (perhaps 6 mm) wide every time it passes through the log, so that when a tree is sawn into one inch planks nearly 25% of it is converted straight away into sawdust. When account is taken of the volume of wavy edge, cracked and knotted pieces, plus the waste that even the most economical carpenter makes, the amount of a tree that ultimately finds its way into a construction is sometimes as low as 30%. But even this is better than my first attempt at 'conversion'!

Chapter Six

TIMBERS

Prior to the seventeenth century the village carpenters and carvers in Britain worked almost exclusively in oak with an occasional excursion into yew, ash, beech, birch, elm or holly for special occasions, or where they had noticed a particular property of one of these timbers to be more suitable than oak for the work in hand. In the latter part of the seventeenth century and the first quarter of the eighteenth the even texture of walnut, which had been introduced into this country by returning crusaders, appeared more suitable for the developments taking place in furniture design and in the same period the first consignments of mahogany began to arrive from the West Indies. The proneness of walnut to attack by woodworm led the first true cabinet makers—Thomas Chippendale (1718–1779), George Hepplewhite (died 1786) and Thomas Sheraton (1751–1806)—to favour mahogany for their art and this wood remained popular* for furniture of the best quality for nearly two centuries.

Gradually, though, a transformation took place in the timber trade. Larch, one of the fast growing softwoods,† became known during the seventeenth century and was planted as a crop towards the end of the eighteenth. By the mid nineteenth century this timber became available in some quantities for manufacturing or building purposes and by the commencement of the Second World War larch or other softwoods were

*This timber and other related red woods are not now popular as the dust created by sawing, planing etc. has been found to be carcinogenic.

†'Softwoods' are resinous woods derived from coniferous trees, whereas 'hardwoods' are derived from the deciduous broad-leaved trees. So far as carving is concerned the terms are confusing, some hardwoods being much easier to work than soft ones.

being imported from Russia, Sweden, Finland or Canada into this country at the rate of thirteen tons to every one of hardwood. Nowadays, as we have seen, hardwood is almost unobtainable in prime and seasoned condition in bulk, although there is—and always will be— plenty of oddments about in various conditions for our kind of work.

The softwoods have been carved for a variety of purposes and at present these timbers, machine sanded and treated with polyurethane varnishes, are extremely fashionable for furniture. They are, however, difficult to carve as they tend to splinter when cut across the grain with any but the sharpest, thinnest-edged, tools, and as they cannot be compared with the majority of hardwoods in durability as well as working characteristics they have been omitted from the following tables of suggested carving woods. These tables are in fact restricted entirely to the hardwoods of the northern hemisphere which grow well in Britain and can be replaced, in line with my suggestion at the beginning of the previous chapter, in the course of time.

In a situation of restricted supply it is not very helpful to recommend particular timbers for carving or to provide firm rules about the suitability of any one for work of a special nature. Some indications can be gleaned from the lists of past and present uses included in Table 1 and a great deal of pleasure will be obtained from exploring the nature of each as pieces become available. Timbers such as poplar and alder have not been included as they are not highly regarded by carvers, although they have other uses.

TABLE I

(*opposite and pages 88 to 93*)

**The Propagation, Seasoning
Characteristics and Uses of
the Common British Hardwoods**

	ASH (European) *FRAXINUS EXCELSIOR*	BEECH (European) *FAGUS SYLVATICA*
PROPAGATION AND SEASONING	From seed; germination in second spring. Loamy soil; likes lime or alkaline peat (Norfolk). Best mixed with denser trees which shade the soil. Not in hedgerows. Grows to 100 ft; diameter 2–5 ft. At its best from 50 years, but for many purposes pollarded at 15. Seasons rapidly without much tendency to crack.	From 'mast' or nuts, many of which will be found empty even after a hot summer. Shallow rooting with wide radius making it unsuitable for hedgerows. Prefers chalk and limestone soils in warm parts where the drainage is also good. Grows to 100 or 150 ft; diameter averages 4 ft; 200–300 years. Dries quickly but liable to check split and warp.
CHARACTERISTICS	White to light brown. Grain straight with pronounced annual rings. Sapwood and heart not clearly defined (sapwood prone to woodworm). Good steam bending properties. Easy to work and takes good finish. Sometimes splinters across the grain. Moderate blunting of tools; greenwood easily split with wedges etc. Wavy grain characteristic of old trees (ram's horn or rammy).	White or pale brown, darkening later and without much character sawn T + T. Marked medullary rays on radial cut. Straight grain, fine even texture. Moderate blunting of tools; greenwood easily split. Susceptible to woodworm. No clear distinction between sap and heartwood.
TRADITIONAL USES	Irreplaceable where spring and resilience are required—axe and hammer handles, tennis rackets, hockey sticks, gardening tools, cart shafts, farm implements, ladders, motor car bodies (Morris Minor Estate), aeroplanes. Demand exceeds supply and timber is imported from Europe, America and Japan.	Much used for furniture manufacture in recent years and imported in large quantities. Piano parts and other musical instruments, boot heels, lasts, bobbins, rollers, spools, tent pegs, car bodies, aeroplanes (The World War 2 Mosquito). Non striking tool handles, mallets. For plywood manufacture. Turns well.

	BIRCH *BETULA VERRUCOSA* or *PUBESCENS*	CHESTNUT (Sweet) *CASTANEA SATIVA*
PROPAGATION AND SEASONING	By seed, 20% of which should germinate in 2–3 weeks if sown when ripe. Dislikes shade, but grows well in open woodlands on poor sandy soil or marshy areas. Grows to the limit of tree line on mountains. Quick growing—50 to 70 ft in 30 years but rarely exceeds this. Air dries fast with tendency to warp and proneness to fungus attack—use thick sticks and narrow airy piles.	By seed in S.E. of Britain but seeds are unreliable further north. Mild climate and fertile soil. Will not flourish in wet conditions, heavy soil or chalk. Grows to 100 ft or more with 20 ft or more of clear bole 6 ft in diameter. Slow seasoning; stains in contact with iron.
CHARACTERISTICS	White to light brown, plain and straight grained. Strong and works easily, although it is sometimes woolly. Mild tool blunting; greenwood easily split. Turns well. Liable to attack by woodworm.	Closely resembles oak in colour and texture, but lacks the medullary rays. The grain of older trees often runs in a spiral formation making the timber useless for structural work. At best up to 60 years but often cropped at 15 when it splits with exceptional ease making excellent fence posts, palings etc. Prone to woodworm attack, sapwood in particular.
TRADITIONAL USES	Small logs only, but extensively used for chair and furniture parts, cotton reels, spools, toys and general turnery. Used extensively for plywood and dowelling.	Since medieval times as a substitute for oak where strength is not necessary. Furniture, barrels, kitchen utensils, turnery. Hop poles, split fencing, gates. Not for veneer or plywood.

	ELM *ULMUS PROCERA* (English) *GLABRA* (Wych)	HORNBEAM *CARPINUS BETULUS*
PROPAGATION AND SEASONING	Profusion of seeds which are rarely fertile north of Spain. In England by transplanted suckers (Wych elm may grow from seed in England). May be found on hills in Scotland but prefers the richer, warmer valleys of the south. Classic hedgerow tree. May live 500 years and grow to 150 ft with a diameter of 5 to 8 ft. Rapid seasoning with marked tendency to warp.	From seeds which do not germinate before second spring unless planted as soon as ripe. Northern limit is Norfolk. Rich loam or clay soil. Good hedgerow tree, but not long lived. Grows 50 ft, 3–4 ft diameter but often with low branches. Seasons easily. Characteristic of Epping Forest.
CHARACTERISTICS	Pink or creamy coloured turning to brown when dry. Coarse grain, often twisted making splitting difficult. Sapwood lighter in colour and clearly distinct—up to 2 inches. Continental elm is straighter than English and the timber from the wych variety is paler, finer and stronger. Marked resistance to moisture. Good for steam bending. Twisted grain makes for difficult planing, saw binding and splitting. Holds nails particularly well.	Plain timber, white and with fine texture. Exceptionally dense, tough and resistant to splitting. Best worked in green state. Ultimately takes good finish.
TRADITIONAL USES	A heavy duty timber used for wharfs, ships' keels, gunwales etc. Farm buildings, weather boarding, wheelbarrows, cartwheel hubs, pumps, garden sheds. Chair seats and turnery. Coffins. Not used for plywood or veneer.	Exceptional toughness makes this timber useful for cogs on mill-wheels, pulley blocks, wood screws, plane blocks, mallets and tools generally. Piano parts, turnery. Flooring. Makes best charcoal.

	HORSE CHESTNUT *AESCULUS HIPPOCASTANUM*	LIME *TILIA VULGARIS*
PROPAGATION AND SEASONING	By seed—easy. Best in warm sheltered situations, but not fussy. Grows to 100 ft or more and 5 ft diameter. Seasons easily with loss of colour.	By layering. Seeds rarely ripen in Britain. Generally planted for ornamental purposes. Withstands soot and smoke. May live over 300 years and grow to 120 ft, diameter 4 ft. Seasons rapidly with some tendency to distort.
CHARACTERISTICS	Very plain white timber, soft and fairly brittle. Takes clear smooth finish with sharp, thin edged tools. Sometimes woolly when wet. Difficult splitting. No distinct heartwood. Liable to woodworm attack.	Soft and creamy coloured. No pronounced markings. Exceptionally easy cutting in either direction with sharp thin edged tools, but difficult to split. Susceptible to woodworm.
TRADITIONAL USES	Not much used in timber trade. Exceptional whiteness makes it useful for dairy utensils, rollers, spools etc. Fruit storage trays and other food containers. May be good for turning and carving.	Exceptional for carving—favoured by Grinling Gibbons. Musical instruments, toys, turnery, kitchen utensils, knitting needles, artificial limbs, shy balls at fairgrounds.

	OAK *QUERCUS ROBUR* and *PETRAEA*	PLANE *PLATANUS ACERIFOLIA*
PROPAGATION AND SEASONING	By acorn, some of which may throw out two or more seedlings. Deep warm fertile soil up to the S. of Scotland. Will grow up to 130 ft and live for over 1000 years. Produces no acorns for 60 years. Slow seasoning. Marked tendency to split and check and discolour.	By seed. Dislikes lime soils, but does not object to soot and smoke. A 'town' tree. Not grown as timber crop. Grows to 100 ft; diameter 3–4 ft. Seasons rapidly with tendency to warp.
CHARACTERISTICS	Exceptional strength. Pale yellow turning brown later. Marked medullary rays. Distinct sapwood—very prone to woodworm and death watch beetle—nearly 2 inches thick. Moderate blunting of tools, difficult splitting. Shallow plane blade setting (20° or less) often required. Corrosive effect on metals, particularly lead. Best timber from specimens over 200 years old.	Similar in colour and markings to beech, but medullary rays darker and more pronounced. Little distinction between heart and sapwood, but sometimes the centre core is discoloured. Works cleanly and easily. Timber sawn radially may be sufficiently decorative to be termed 'lacewood'.
TRADITIONAL USES	Heavy constructional work, flooring, wheels, gates, garden furniture, weatherboarding. Ship building—blocks, slipways, beams, keels, rudders etc. Plywood and veneer. Roots used for knife handles.	Cabinet work, fancy boxes, panelling, coach sides— decorative work generally.

	SYCAMORE *ACER PSEUDOPLATANUS*	WALNUT *JUGLANS REGIA*
PROPAGATION AND SEASONING	From seed as far north as Lancashire and Yorkshire. Thrives on all but the poorest soils and is resistant to salt spray and industrial fumes. Grows to 100 ft in 60 years, diameter 5 ft. Rarely exceeds 200 years in age. Air seasons well, but prone to staining. May mark where stickers have been—kilning advised.	From seed, but nuts do not often ripen in England. Dislikes hard frost, heavy clay and poor sandy soil. Requires room and will not stand shade. Grows up to 100 ft, diameter 2–3 or even up to 5 ft. Slow seasoning.
CHARACTERISTICS	Yellowish white with fine even texture and natural lustre. Works evenly and well, but where the grain is wavy requires low angle plane blades. Moderate blunting of tools and medium ease of splitting in green condition. Not suitable for exterior work. Sometimes stained grey and sold as 'harewood'.	Greyish brown with dark streaks. Sapwood is light and the centre of the heartwood noticeably darker than the rest. The colour fades in sunlight to a dull brown. Timber stains heavily in contact with metal. Heavily figured textures appear in burrs and branch junctions. Root timber is especially suitable for decorative veneers. Not too easy to split. Sapwood particularly attractive to woodworm. Does not warp and cuts cleanly in any direction.
TRADITIONAL USES	Kitchen and dairy utensils, chopping boards, bread boards and general turnery—rolling pins, butter pats etc. Large rollers for textile industry and mangles. Popular for light coloured furniture—especially figured logs. Veneers. Violin backs.	Decorative furniture and turned goods of all kinds. Interior panelling, veneers. Freedom from movement and warpage makes it suitable for aircraft propellers and gunstocks.

TIMBERS AVAILABLE IN SMALL SIZES ONLY

APPLE   *Malus sylvestris*
             Creamy, dense and fine. Used for mallets, skittle balls
             and fancy work. Turns well.

BOX   *Buxus sempervirens*
             Creamy white and hard. Used for drawing instru-
             ments, wood engravers' blocks, small turnery and
             parts of musical instruments.

CHERRY   *Prunus avium*
             Used for high grade furniture, decorative pieces,
             veneers, turnery and woodwind instruments.
             (recorders etc.)

HOLLY   *Ilex aquifolium*
             Hard and white. Used for inlay, marquetry, small
             turnery, wood engraving blocks. When stained black
             as a substitute for ebony.

LABURNUM   *Laburnum anagyroides*
             Dark with pronounced sapwood. Used for decorative
             work, veneers, inlays, knife handles and woodwind
             instruments (recorders, flutes etc.).

PEAR   *Pyrus communis*
             Pinkish brown, fine texture. Used for drawing
             instruments, wood engraving and printing blocks, saw
             handles and small turnery.

FIELD MAPLE *Acer campestre*
             Similar to sycamore.

TABLE 2

Average Weights and Shrinkages
of the Common British Hardwoods

	Average weight per cubic foot (lbs)			Percentage of shrinkage from wet to 12% moisture content	
	Green	Seasoned	% Loss	Radial	Tangential
ASH	52	43	17	4·5	7·0
BEECH	60	45	25	4·5	9·5
BIRCH	60	41	32	5·0	8·0
CHESTNUT (Sweet)	65	34	48	3·0	5·5
ELM	65	34	48	4·5	6·5
HORNBEAM	62	47	24	5·0	7·0
HORSE-CHESTNUT	58	32	45	2·0	3·0
LIME	62	34	45	5·0	7·5
OAK	67	45	33	4·0	7·5
PLANE	61	39	36	4·0	9·5
SYCAMORE	57	38	25	2·5	5·5
WALNUT	51	40	22	3·0	5·5
Available in small sizes only					
APPLE		44			
BOX		57			
CHERRY		38			
HOLLY		49			
LABURNUM		53			
PEAR		44			

TABLE 3

North American Counterparts of British Hardwoods
(Found mostly in the eastern States and south east Canada)

Average seasoned weight in lbs per cubic foot in brackets.

ASH (white)	*Fraxinus americana.* Slightly less dense.	(41)
ASH (Oregon)	Inferior in strength, otherwise good.	
BASSWOOD (LIME)	*Tilia americana.* Softer.	(27)
BEECH	*Fagus grandifolia.* Similar.	(45)
BIRCH (yellow)	*Betula alleghaniensis.* Harder and darker.	(43)
BIRCH (paper or white)	*Betula papyrifera.* Equivalent of European.	
CHERRY (wild black)	*Prunus serotina.* Similar to European, more freely available	(36)
ELM (rock)	*Ulmus thomasi.* Lighter brown, straighter grain, much tougher.	(49)
ELM (white)	*Ulmus americana.* Straighter grain, tougher.	(38)
MAPLE (black)	*Acer niger.* Resembles English sycamore, but harder. (N.B. American sycamore, *Platanus occidentalis*, is a different timber).	(45)
MAPLE (soft)	*Acer rubrum* (red); *A. saccharinum* (silver); *A. macrophyllum* (Pacific). Soft timbers, otherwise similar.	(38)
OAK (white)	*Quercus* (various). Resembles European.	(47)
OAK (red)	*Quercus* (various). Red brown and coarser.	(41–48)
WALNUT (black)	*Juglans nigra.* Resembles European, but darker. More freely available, especially in large sizes.	(35–42)

For further information—particularly on the many exotic hardwoods of Central and South America imported into the U.S.A.—see Bibliography.

Chapter Seven

COPING

A friend recently said to me that one of his colleagues responsible for teaching carving always started his students making bowls, believing that if they had learned to carve a good hollow and a matching humped form they could manage anything. If I had been started that way *as an exercise* I should probably never have picked up a carving tool again, but, nevertheless, there is perhaps something in what this teacher says, and, having commenced carving bowls long beforehand from the love of the forms, I was able to weigh up these remarks more coolly. Watching some of my own students at work recently has confirmed the wisdom of them—a good, clean, simple hollow form is really difficult to achieve and very demanding upon the sense of feel as well as the use of tools.

From experience I now start with a fine outline drawn in pen and two or three intermediate lines representing stages in the progress of the work. At each stage I try to obtain a good hollow form indicative of the final curvature, though I do not stop to clean up the surface. The work commences with a wide drilled hole (*opposite top*) in the centre and the largest deep straight gouge (Nos. 8, 9 or 10) that can be handled in the space, proceeding round in a regular formation of swooping furrows.

When, after several concentric rings of orderly gouging, the first intermediate line is reached, an assessment is made of the curvature and the depth of the hollow. Very likely the drilled hole is still evident, but with a stick across the top of the bowl and a ruler held vertically down to the rim of this hole the depth can be measured and the thickness remaining can be compared with the distance still to be cut away on the top surface between this first line and the final one. If the curvature is already generally correct, clearing the remaining intermediate stages should leave a bottom thickness slightly less than that intended for the rim. If there is a real discrepancy between the likely thickness of the base

96

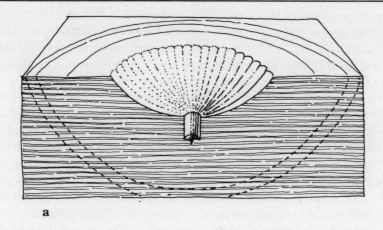

a

b

Hollowing out the interior of a bowl.

and the rim, adjustment of the curvature—deeper or shallower—must be made during the cutting of the next stage.

Sometimes it is possible to carry out the entire second stage using the same large straight gouge, but the curvature may by now be already too

steep for a gouge of this kind to move through it without the handle
jamming against the top edge. When this happens it is necessary to use
both a straight and a bent gouge to complete each cut; very likely a
salmon bend (Nos. 14, 15 or 16) will do, but sometimes it is already
necessary to work in the bottom with a spoon bit (Nos. 26 or 27).

Once a spoon bit has been resorted to, I find it best to concentrate for a
while on the bottom of the bowl and to cut right down to the final
measure, usually, as I have indicated already, leaving a bottom which is
thinner than the rim. Sometimes the base may need to be equal to the
rim, but if it is thicker it will 'come up to meet the eye' and always feel
wrong in weight.

When the bottom has been thoroughly opened out, cutting back the
sides with straight and salmon bend gouges to the final line is an easy and
pleasant task. The bowl suddenly opens up and the true quality of the
curvature reveals itself for the first time. The flutings of the deep gouges
used so far add to the fascination of the form, but they are unlikely to be
accurate or rhythmical enough to leave in the finished bowl and in any case
would restrict its use to a decorative object as they bruise fruit and
interfere with serving. The value of a fine pen outline, rather than a thick
chalk one, now becomes evident as the sharp edge of the gouge is set
exactly on this line at the commencement of each downward cut.

The ridges between the flutings can now be removed very easily by
the use of shallow gouges (Nos. 4, 5, 14 or 15) without the mallet. At this
stage I usually prop the bowl up at an angle so that I am pushing into it,
rather than downwards with operative elbow cocked high above my
shoulder. And here, in particular, the sharpness of tool matters very
much; it must be razor sharp with a lovely shallow polished bevel enabling
it to pare away the wood in thin slices like a plane. The fingers are feeling
the curvature all the time and on the look out for the slightest
unconformity, so often a slight straightening of the curve as though the
bowl had been pushed in from the outside. Very good light is essential at
this stage of the work.

At one time I used to turn the bowl over as soon as the interior was
finished to deal with the back, leaving the rim until last. This was a
mistake as it became extremely difficult to hold the bowl still for the
finishing touches and I was prevented from using such delightful tools

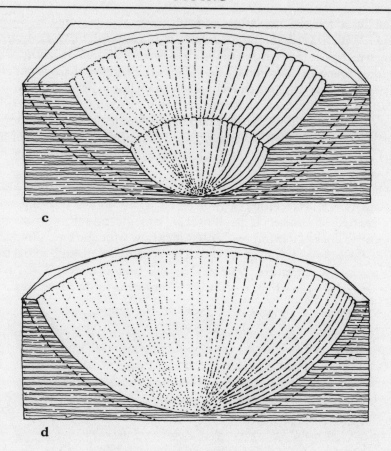

c

d

Hollowing out the interior of a bowl.

as the spokeshaves on the rim where they could have been most useful. Anyway, work on the rim commences now as soon as the logs are away and the fine triangles left between the saw cuts have been planed down to the line. The bowl is still quite stable.

The importance of rim forms to the sculptural quality of bowls was stressed in Chapter Two (pages 26 and 27) and some of the range of

possibilities for one curvature and thickness of bowl only is shown
below. With regard to rounded rims it is essential to work from a
bevel which is at right angles to the cross section of the bowl, otherwise
the form becomes distorted by the difference of angles at the inner and
outer edges. The work is helped by an accurate line to bevel down to and
is carried out with spokeshaves (round sole spokeshave on the inside,
flat sole on the outside) or a very sharp block plane and files. As the upper
edge is likely to be slightly scratched and dented whilst the back of the
bowl is being carved away the final surfacing of the rim with a fine file
and sandpaper is left to the end.

The need to mark out the bottom of a bowl while the block of wood is
still square was also learned early on and it is now done at the same time
as a matter of course. I do, however, provide myself with several
concentric lines as it is impossible to judge how wide the base should be
before the interior has been carved. The business of making radial saw
cuts across the curvature (page 22) has also been abandoned as I now
have several gouges which are capable of removing timber at an amazing

Some of the variety of rim forms which could be used on
bowls which are otherwise similar in shape.

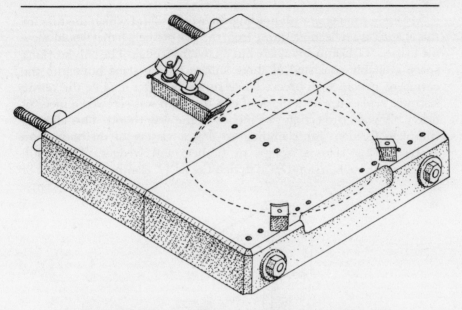

Clamping base for bowls. The base measures 18″ × 18″ × 3″ (46 × 46 × 7·5 cm) and can expand to accommodate larger bowls. It can also serve as a vice and is ideal for sharpening saws when two deeper pieces of stout timber, notched to drop over the screw threads, are let into the centre. The moveable stops for the bowl pivot on iron rods and the blocks are faced with leather. The base itself is either clamped to the bench or screwed firmly through the front half. A similar device could be made from thick plywood without the longitudinal screws.

speed—indeed my chippings have sufficient thickness to serve as an excellent slow burning fuel!

There is, though, the need to devise some arrangements for holding the upturned bowl still, otherwise the work becomes extremely irritating and noisy. I have tried a variety of ways of doing this of which the 'clamping base' shown above, based on the principle of a chuck or jaw, is the most sophisticated. This can be clamped onto any bench and is particularly useful for the final planing.

My early problems with holding the work still (of which the title for this chapter is a reflection!) arose from the lack of a bench that would allow me to use a 'G' clamp anywhere but on the front edge. The only working space available consisted of three square paving slabs built into the corner of a room with breeze block supports. After a while the centre slab was replaced with a block of elm to which was screwed a piece of heavy plywood projecting two inches all the way round. This allowed complete freedom for clamping so that a variety of methods were evolved using clamps, scraps of timber, and wedges. There still remained, though, a number of difficulties as 'G' clamps have a habit of

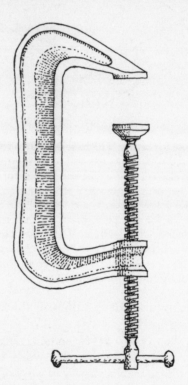

'G' clamp. Only the larger ones, 6″ or 8″ (150 or 200 mm), are useful in bowl making or sculpture.

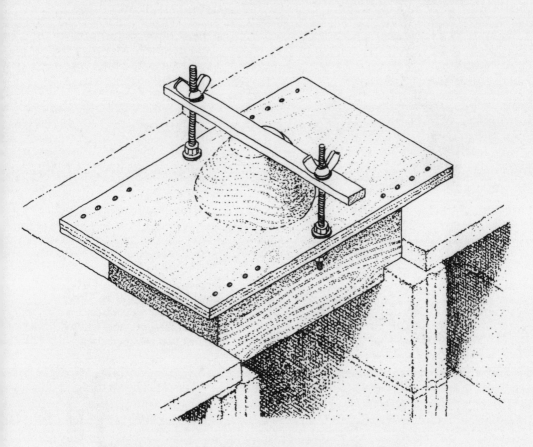

Interior work bench with adjustable clamp. Wider objects can be accommodated by setting the screws diagonally.

continually unscrewing themselves from the vibration of carving and often have to be fixed in positions which make the work awkward to get at. The bench is now fitted with an adjustable clamp shown above which is equally useful for bowls or sculptures.

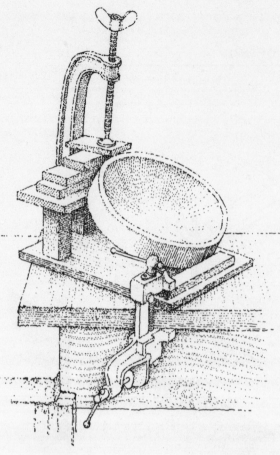

IMPROVISED METHODS

a) bowl tilted against a raised platform which allowed a 'G' clamp to grip the back edge.

b) planing the back of a large bowl. The work is done down the far side whilst the body presses the bowl against two clamped stops.

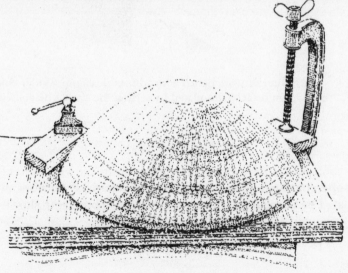

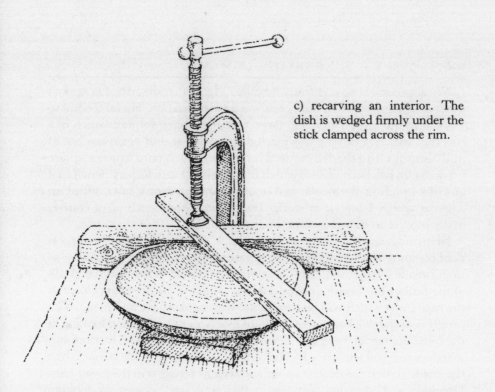

c) recarving an interior. The dish is wedged firmly under the stick clamped across the rim.

d) carving an exterior. The work is done on the far side and the piece of timber under the clamp prevents the bowl from jumping with each knock.

My approach is now entirely flexible. The bench described is against the south facing wall of a 'sunroom'—a lovely situation, but far too hot to work at in the middle of many days. Outside I have another bench in a sun trap which is often a sheer delight to work at, but again too hot in mid-summer. In a shaded corner I have a tree trunk onto which a square piece of elm has been nailed, which makes a most satisfactory bench as it absorbs much of the noise, and another shorter trunk sawn off at an angle at which I can sit to work. This latter tilted bench is, of course, easily moved so that it is sometimes used inside.

Returning now to working on the back of a bowl, I use the largest possible gouge radially down the curvature, attempting to maintain—as in the inside—a methodically concentric approach. When the main bulk of the timber has been removed a flatter gouge is sought to get closer to the final form which will be completed with spokeshave and plane. The progress of the work requires constant assessment by feel and looking at the bowl the correct way up. Not all bowls require an even section, but there is a marked tendency for the outside curve to be made steeper than the inside so that too much timber and weight remains in the lower half. Divergence of the two surfaces in this way can be seen by looking carefully down at the rim. Excess is sometimes left in the lower half of a bowl from anxiety about making the base too narrow. Obviously a base *can* be made too narrow, but by critical assessment a diameter at this point will be found which is visually and practically stable as well as being reasonable in section and weight.

When as much gouge work has been done as seems possible—and I finish off to some extent paring by hand to remove the high ridges— work is started radially down the form with a spokeshave or small block plane. The latter tool is useful near the base and the rim as its longer sole in front of and behind the cutting edge provides more area to ride over the main part of the curvature. Surform tools can also be useful before the final planing.

Finally, when the section of the bowl has been approved by eye and feel, the base usually requires a little planing to remove pen marks. This is most easily done using a finely set block plane in several directions and if the tool is properly sharpened it is easier working across the grain than with it.

5. Three bowls with edges decorated by a pyrographic needle – an instrument which seems to open up endless possibilities. The bottom dish in lime was lettered impromptu with the names of the author's family and dog by Ronald Parsons F.S.D.C. The two smaller dishes were decorated by Susan Green.

6. Two small bowls in oiled (*top*) and burnished elm.

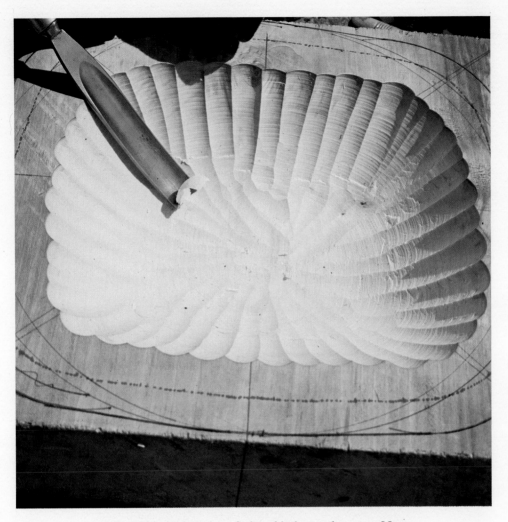

7. Carving the interior of a bowl in horsechestnut. Note the coarse quality of the initial gougework executed rapidly with a no. 8, $1\frac{1}{4}''$ gouge. Nearer the line a no. 7 tool will be used less vigorously and the surface will be finished without a mallet with a no. 6 or 5. In the picture a curved tool is commencing to turn the corner at the bottom of the bowl.

8. Small carving in a mahogany by the author. Perhaps no more than a tactile toy, but very satisfying to make. Length, 8″ (20 cm).

We now have a bowl with shallow paring marks inside, a smoothed rim and an outside with very slight facets from the spokeshave and plane. These tool marks can easily be removed with scrapers, files and sandpaper, but, if they are clean and regular, do we need to bother? This is a difficult point to answer; generally I leave them alone, but have occasionally removed them when some shape or grain pattern seems to need to be smooth. Bowls carved from green wood certainly need a light rub over with very fine sand or flour paper after they have dried out to remove fine whiskers of grain, but this does not disturb the feel or look of the toolmarks. They will also benefit from rewetting, which raises the grain like sharp bristles, followed by resanding with fine flour paper—an operation which can well be repeated several times during the seasoning period until a smooth burnished surface is achieved. The burnish can be further enhanced by rubbing with a smooth hard stone.

OTHER SURFACE TREATMENTS

Being concerned in my own work and in these pages far more with the form of objects than any pattern or texture on their surfaces, I must say straight away that to me pronounced grain can sometimes prove a distraction and treatments which draw attention to it may be highly undesirable. If this attitude sounds uncompromising (and almost the reverse of current feeling in the woodworking business as a whole— especially turning) I can only plead that I have worked for over twenty years with students of pottery who so often coat the worst of their products with their best glazes in an attempt to cover up their mistakes!

Now, with this awful warning out of the way I can safely add that as a rule I am as enchanted as everyone else with the grain patterns of timber, the incredible variety of them, their richness, and the way that they so often follow the contours of forms, adding to everything as they wander over ridges and hollows. It is again a matter of control, preference, and the importance of every aspect of a product contributing to the rightness of the whole. After all, there are plenty of timbers where the grain hardly shows—lime and sycamore for instance—which can be used where a strong linear pattern on the surface would seem inappropriate, and others, like the lovely elm wood, where strident lines and dark bands flow across every inch. The 'right' form must be seen in the wood before work commences and for this reason, even if it is quite unnecessary for accuracy in the work, it is advisable to thoroughly plane off the top surface at least of strange pieces of wood before work is started, for the plane brings out grain in a way that cannot be matched by any other tool.

Although it may often seem desirable to leave a product with the colour, pattern and quality that the tools make on the surface, this is impractical. Wood needs some treatment for the sake of preservation, to prevent moisture continually entering it and drying out and to protect it from dirt, grease or stains. With domestic utensils which are to be used for serving or preparing food this protective element of wood treatment is especially important and it is fortunately possible to make wooden vessels quite impervious to gravy, salad dressings, beetroot, fruit juice and the like without resorting to any form of varnish which might be thought to be unpleasant in contact with food. Cooking oil—olive, sunflower seed etc.—is perfectly adequate protection when rubbed into the wood as soon as it has properly dried out and there can be nothing in this treatment that could be considered harmful.

The initial drying out, as we have seen, takes some months and when oil is first applied* all woods darken in colour considerably. After a period in use, with frequent washing up in cold or warm water (but not detergent), the colour lightens a little, until at some point the wood appears to be absorbing moisture. Then, after it has been allowed to dry out, the wood must be oiled again and it may be necessary to reburnish the surface before this is done. After a great deal of use, with several oilings, the wood begins to assume a rich patina which it seems can be acquired in no other way. The article will now live on to posterity, slowly assuming the character of the dairy and kitchen vessels from the past which are so eagerly sought by the antique trade.

Other wood treatments are designed to make the material impervious *before* any oil or wax is applied to the surface, and, although these

---

*A good method of applying oil is to fill a jam jar with cotton wool and pour some of the oil onto it. When the wool is thoroughly impregnated, wrap it in soft cloth (nylon stocking material is good) and rub the wood vigorously with this pad, ending with a clean rag to remove surplus oil which has not penetrated the wood.

treatments are possibly technically desirable, they do show a hardness of quality, lacking real depth. For instance, there is available a shellac based 'sanding sealer' which is rubbed down to a silky mattness with fine sandpaper after the application has dried to a gloss (polyurethane finishes can be treated in the same way) and the matted surface is then treated with beeswax polish,* furniture cream or oils and vigorously rubbed with a soft cloth to bring out the grain and colour. These treatments may be admirable for sculptures as they can then be cleaned and repolished with ease, but, in some cases, even with these objects, thought should be given to the desirability of leaving the natural surface of the wood alone, reckoning that it will sometimes need to be scrubbed and resanded. Here, as with glazes, there are no rules; each case must be treated on its own merits and tests on scrap pieces of the same wood made beforehand to help in reaching a decision.

There is no need to mention here the preventive treatments for fungus or insect attack or to describe fireproofing measures, varnishes or French polish, as any of this information is readily available in other books.

---

*Beeswax polish is made by melting wax together with turpentine (1 lb of wax to ½ pint turps or 450 g to 0.6 litre) in a tin of boiling water and is applied thinly whilst warm. After the coating has dried it is burnished vigorously with a soft cloth. Good quality furniture cream can be used when necessary to revive the beeswax finish.

Linseed oil also penetrates the wood more satisfactorily when it has been thinned with about 5% of turpentine or white spirit.

Chapter Eight

SCULPTURE—THE TACTILE ART?

The endless possibilities of bowl forms have satisfactorily absorbed the majority of my free time for several years now and I have not been surprised to discover that other craftsmen have also found sufficient scope in making bowls to do it for a livelihood. Some of their forms are freer and more succulent than mine, reflecting perhaps greater experience of the work as well as a difference of personality. Possibly there are dozens engaged in the same way and the work of us all will be clearly distinguishable to anyone with the time to stop and handle our products.

However, once bitten by the fascination of forms in general, others of a more elaborate nature than bowls and probably without any potential use whatsoever—apart from serving as bases for sculptural ideas—are bound to be discovered. This happens to me often as I dig the garden or go for a walk, so that my workroom and the sitting room mantelpiece have become cluttered with pieces of twig, decayed plastic, scraps of bone, old scaffold clamps and the like, which would require some hundreds of free hours each week, not just a few, if more than a handful of them were to be given permanence as sculptures.

In Chapter Two the value was emphasised of disappearing surfaces, which lead the eyes of the observer round the form and make him conscious of the existence of a side he cannot see from where he is standing, and it was suggested that if all the forms and empty spaces of a sculpture contribute to this consciousness of the existence of another side an observer would be impelled either to walk around the object, or, if it is small enough, to pick it up. The curiosity aroused enhances the consciousness of the solidity of an object and in causing bodily movement establishes a degree of vital force or tactile value in it.

It is difficult to make a bowl form that has no tactility at all because neither the inner nor the outer surfaces can be seen in their entirety from any point of view, but there are, nevertheless, degrees of vital force in bowls. Some spring to the hand. With solid forms, where the interior is not exposed, it is a different matter and the contrivance of movement requires conscious thought on the part of the carver. Take for example a rectangular synthetic sponge. It is impossible to deny that this object is three-dimensional as it has height, length and breadth. We are aware from long experience that it has six sides, but from no point of view—despite the fact that we have two eyes aligned stereoscopically—can we see more than three of them or *exactly half the total surface area*.

Stand the sponge upright on a table and give it a slight twist. Looking at it again from one of the narrow sides, we find that we can now see the whole of a narrow face, the top and part of *both* the wider sides disappearing from view in the direction of the twist. So, in the twisted sponge we can actually see from one viewpoint at least four out of six faces, and, although we cannot see the entirety of either of the wider ones, we can see enough of them both to cause us to *move* our heads a little each way to find out where the disappearing surfaces go.

A sponge is not, of course, a particularly interesting object to look at and if we do bother to see where the surfaces go after it has been twisted the new views will be little more enchanting than the first glance. However, we have seen that a change of direction in the cross-section of an object establishes 'movement' at the surface.

The sponge, unfortunately springs back to its original non-tactile shape as soon as we let go of it, so let us now take a piece of wood—five or six inches of 2″ × 2″ or 2″ × 1″* will do—and saw off the opposite corners making new triangular faces down to just beyond the half way. When this has been done take a rasp or knife to the edges of the new triangular faces and begin to merge them into the original surfaces of the timber, sometimes concavely, sometimes convexly. Then set about treating each of the remaining right angular corners of the wood with different degrees of curvature, again merging them into what is left of the flat faces so that the original square or rectangular cross-section is entirely lost.

*One inch = 25.4 mm.

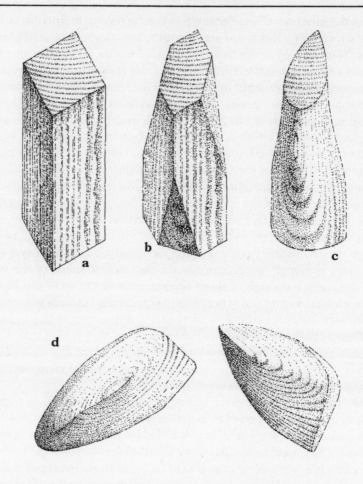

Experiments with sculptural movement: a) 5″ length of 2″ × 2″; b) four opposite corners sawn off; c) sawn corners merged into the original faces; d) end surfaces also treated with varying degrees of curvature; *two views of a complete 'sculpture'*; e) 2″ × 2″ with longer cuts; f) 2″ × 1″ with short cuts.

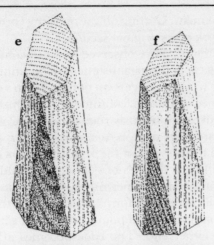

As the work progresses the object becomes increasingly difficult to fix in the vice because it is no longer square in section at any point and it becomes increasingly pleasant to hold. Perhaps it will become so fascinating to hold that it is worth *turning round* in the hand?

When the top and bottom surfaces have also been treated by thorough removal of the corners—again with different degrees of curvature—we will suddenly find that the piece of wood has been translated into a very real piece of sculpture. So leave it around the house and watch what happens—no one will be able to resist picking it up as soon as they set eyes on it!

This is all very exciting. It will have become evident during the work that at even this primitive level of sculptural ideas—equivalent in literature to the subject–verb–object sentence, 'I make sculpture', or in music to the scale of G—there is the possibility of considerable variety and readers will doubtless set about other pieces in timber of different dimensions and with the first cuts of different lengths as soon as possible.

One subtle point that we might notice immediately is the difficulty of imitating the facial curvatures of a twisted sponge in wood. This is because the sponge material is not rigid and in twisting it the cross-section is gently distorted all the way up the height. This point is important, for if we leave any of the original cross-section of the timber in our whittled models they will feel blocklike and not entirely converted to sculptural movement. Cutting off the opposite corners is the quickest way to rid the block of its original section.

Another 'rule' that we have observed so far unconsciously in making these wooden objects is the establishment of 'continuity of surface'. If we have done our work of conversion of the section very thoroughly we will find that the new surface is 'continuous', i.e. a finger can start at one point on it and move continuously round the whole object without ever coming upon a hard edge or stop *from which there is no escape.*

In rounding off the remains of the original corners of the wood it was suggested that different degrees of curvature should be employed, so sandpaper one corner only sufficiently to remove its roughness. This short length of real corner now forms a definite stop to the movement of a finger over the surface at this point, but, as the corner is only short, escape is easy at either end. The edge becomes a firm focus to the movement; it sharpens one shadow area and gives the object crispness, variety and direction of movement without frustration.

The next step in exploring the rule of 'continuity of surface' is to drill a fair sized hole through one of our objects, preferably at a point where the section is reasonably thick, and then to set about uniting this new feature with the rest of the object in such a way that its drilled beginning is entirely lost. Merely sanding away the sharp corners is not sufficient by any means, although perhaps one segment of the circumference at one side may in the end remain as a smoothed edge like the short length of corner left from the original cross-section of the wood. Almost certainly it will be necessary to start by gouging a tapering channel down towards the hole from the opposite end of the object. This will set up some new problems of surface continuity all round, but gradually by similar drastic means much of the surface of one face will begin to move towards the hole, seeking to lead us round to the back. Something similar but different will be needed there too, until eventually the drilled hole is converted from a separate form into one which unites the opposite surfaces into one continuous movement.

When all this has been completed the hole ceases to exist as such; it is now merely a gap between two solid forms which grow around it from either end of the object. The hole is unlikely to remain round and practically nothing of the original surface cut by the drill will still exist.

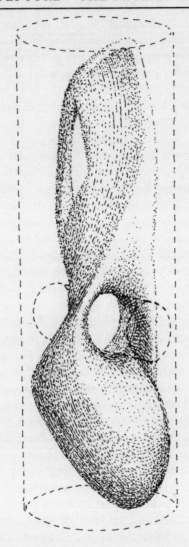

'Continuity of surface'. A drilled hole converted from a separate form into one which unites opposite surfaces into one continuous movement. (A student exercise whittled from a firelog 9″ in length).

It will have added appreciably to the complexity of the surface movements of the object, transformed its sections throughout, and, we hope, contributed substantially to its tactile fascination. Give the finished object to a baby lying awake in a pram and the child's unjaded delight in tactile qualities will quite possibly keep it occupied until the next feed—an amazing lesson in aesthetic appreciation!

SHAPE

Notice, too, that so far the shape of the silhouette of the object has not been mentioned, only the cross-section of the forms. Shape is a two-dimensional phenomenon belonging primarily to the world of painting and graphics, but it is of some concern to the sculptor for before an object is felt it has to attract the attention of the spectator's eyes. In the case of larger sculptures which have to stand in landscapes or among buildings the silhouette from every angle is, of course, extremely important, but, even so, shape does not override the value of form if the sculptor's message is to be put across effectively to a spectator who has been sufficiently intrigued to walk up to it.

Shape or silhouette will be emphasised in the simple experiments we have been talking about as soon as we decide to give them a way up by mounting them on a base like 'real' sculptures. The temptation to do this rather than to leave them simply lying around is understandable and very much part of the tradition of displaying sculptures in exhibitions or on the mantelshelf. With larger and heavier objects it is inevitable—they must stand still somewhere and be safely anchored, but, unless they form part of a building this does not prevent them from being considered and seen completely in the round as well as in shape.

The two-dimensions of 'shape', in contrast to the three-dimensions of 'tactile form', are of course more easily understood and far more widely appreciated at a time like the present when, as was suggested in Chapter Two (page 25), the visual and intellectual aspects of the arts are given saturation coverage and the tactile is frustrated. The figure opposite, showing a poster found ouside a recent exhibition of sculpture is illuminating—WARNING . . . SCULPTURES . . . PLEASE DO NOT TOUCH—and the dominance of the visual approach can frequently be witnessed in the way people talk about craftwork, especially glass and pottery.

WARNING

SOME OF THE
SCULPTURES
ARE FRAGILE
AND
PRECARIOUS

THIS COULD
BE DANGEROUS
TO CHILDREN

Please Do Not Touch

RULES OR LAWS?

Now, have I been expounding grammatical rules conjured up by men to confound sculptors, or laws which arise fundamentally from the natural world? This could be a tricky question because the tendency among students—quite rightly—is to run a mile from anyone who proposes rules which might interfere with the free play of the imagination.

Well, where do the theories of musical composition begin—with rules propounded by the Contrapuntalists and the Romantics or the frequencies of sound vibrations? Did theories of pictorial composition begin with the Golden Section of the Greeks and the perspective of Brunelleschi, or the observed appearances of natural phenomena? Is colour theory based on the writings of people like Ostwald and Munsell, or the results of Newton's investigations into the properties of light? And do we put verbs in our sentences because teachers told us to?

No, the answers are obvious. These theories concerning art stem directly from observations of natural laws which have been observed, formulated, and digested by artists in their formative years, buried in the subconscious during the first stages of maturity and finally pushed aside to make room for their own discoveries—their style—in the latter years of their lives. In the works of Beethoven and Van Gogh this evolutionary path seems to me to be wonderfully clear—can anyone complain of thwarted, rule-bound imaginations at work in Opus 135 or The Cornfield?

But, the fact remains that despite all that is written about theories concerning the arts which play upon our visual and aural senses, practically nothing is ever said about those related to the sense of touch. The rules that I have proposed—those of 'disappearing' and 'continuous' surfaces—are most clearly observed in human and animal anatomy and are discussed in a round about way in the sciences of structures and material strengths. For example, the bones of birds are sometimes regarded as nature's finest products in terms of mechanical ratio of weight to strength, and, as these same bones display to the very highest degrees the operation of the rules suggested, it may well be possible that these are not aesthetic rules so much as natural laws.

However, to suggest that such rules or laws govern the whole world of sculpture would of course be as ridiculous as demanding that all paintings should be conceived in terms of perspective or all music as fugues. These rules concerning the grammar of tactile forms are merely part of the language of sculpture, but they form an essential element in the early training of anyone who is engaged in three-dimensional work. So PLEASE TOUCH.

Chapter Nine

SEEING

The next time you have a free day go to the Tate Gallery as early as you can and ask one of the attendants if you may borrow a pile of nice clean bricks that used to be displayed there. If he says yes, move them into the room where Degas' Little Dancer is shown, mark out on the floor beside it a square of equal size to the plinth and build up the bricks within these lines to the height of the figure. Now begin to draw the figure with chalk on each face of the brick pile as though you were a sculptor preparing to carve such a figure out of a block of marble. You will be amazed how difficult the work is and how long it will be before you feel really confident about marking out the first large volumes of material to be cut away by your assistants. Eventually, though, after hours of cross-checking, measuring and hard looking, you will be able to mark up the block reasonably accurately ready for them to start cutting.

This is a straightforward exercise in seeing the figure three-dimensionally and envisaging it within the confines of a block of material, exactly, in fact, as I saw my first oval bowl within a boss of elmwood lying in a field. If the task seems difficult it is because with this figure we have plunged in at the deep end, for no one, I think, would contemplate carving such sheer dynamic elegance out of a solid material. It is essentially a modelled figure, worked in clay on a metal armature, moulded in plaster and then cast in bronze.

But the exercise will do no harm, and, even if you fail to get permission to use the bricks, it is worth attempting to visualise the figure broadly in these terms. For a start, look at the placing of the feet and the taut forms Degas discovered in the dancer's legs. The flowing movement and section changes will remind you immediately of the experiments we made from wood and as you struggle to interpret the form of the upper part of the body, the arms, the head and the hair, you

EDGAR DEGAS. (1834–1917) 'The Little Dancer'. 1880.
Height 36″ (91.5 cm) (Tate Gallery, London).

will find the same forces at work. Large planes (such as we might have been able to saw off our blocks) spiral up the figure and through the linkage of the hands at the back we are brought unceasingly round the model. From the side the tilt of the neck whips down the arms and the angle of the right leg is picked up again by the tilt of the chest. The fabric skirt and bow, contrasting with the bronze in form and texture, are masterly touches.

Degas would, of course, have been upset by this cold analysis of his sculpture. Such elementary considerations lay deep down in his subconscious, for his vision had been sharpened years beforehand and kept alive at the highest level of intensity by incessant work in pencil, pen, pastel, paint and clay. He hoped we should see his figure as the epitome of a young dancer—elegant, refined, dignified, confident, alive and supremely beautiful. He succeeded. The first impact of this profound sculpture has lasted in me undiminished for thirty years and the image always comes to mind at the mention of 'ballet' or 'dancer'. Degas 'took me over' and this is what art is about.

So, if we are to succeed, our first problem as woodcarvers is to see our images within the pieces of wood before we begin to carve them. To do this effectively we have to retrain our visual apparatus to add the third dimension to everything we look at.

*   *   *

As with the first bowl interior, the first carving will probably arise not so much from what you might like to carve eventually as from what wood you have available now. With these pieces in mind the search for an idea is narrowed and it is certainly helpful if the source is inanimate—an actual object from the hedgerow or the beach—which you can bring into the workshop to handle frequently while the work is in progress.

A helpful idea is to make an open-sided box to scale with a selected piece of timber and large enough to contain the object with some spare space at one end. This takes a little juggling, but the figure opposite shows such a box measuring inside $1\cdot2'' \times 1\cdot5'' \times 2\cdot0''$ which was just large enough to contain a particular clay model. The interior of the box is equivalent to a piece of suitable carving timber reduced to the scale of one

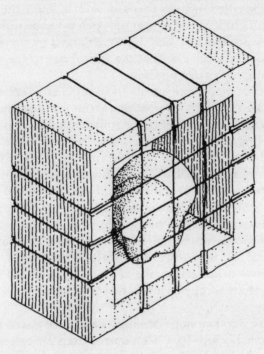

Three-dimensional viewing or enlarging box.

fifth, so that we are considering here the model being enlarged in the carving by five times (see Plate 8).

The spare space at the top is important because it means that some of the wood will remain uncarved and therefore rectangular in section for clamping firmly to the bench throughout the preliminary stages. Before the forms can be completed this surplus wood will have to be sawn off, but its presence throughout the major part of the work will be an untold blessing. As we have noted before, large pieces of wood remain still without clamps and, from this point of view at least, are much easier to work.

When a suitable scale of enlargement has been worked out and a box made, the next step is to cut small slots at equal intervals around the front and back edges with a fine saw and to bind the box—object enclosed—with black cotton so that the open sides are now divided into squares. These squares are then drawn, enlarged by the relevant scale, on the faces of the timber so that the main lines of the object can be transferred into the correct positions.

This sounds as though we are about to begin an exercise in copying, but this is not necessarily so. Something about the form and possibly the shape of the object has appealed to us sufficiently for us to want to carve it, so that our first job is to get at these features as accurately as possible. Later, after the main features of the form have been obtained in the carving, the original model will probably be put on one side and an element of interpretation or translation of the qualities of the form will come about in the work as we concentrate upon its completion.

A painter has something of the same problem in translating small free sketches into more substantial finished works. The final picture is sometimes tired and unworthy of its lively beginnings, and, where this unfruitful situation has arisen, the cause is to be found in the artist's inaccurate understanding of what he had originally seen in his mind and captured in the sketch.

Again, many wood or stone carvings—and I have seen this approach recommended in books—have been started from a rough sketch in chalk on one face of the block. The surplus material is then sawn off and the actual carving started by rounding the four corners. But this is a two-dimensional 'graphic' approach which is generally still evident in the finished work. It is not three-dimensional thinking which might result in a tactile sculpture.

So time must be spent in the preliminary stages. Despite the eagerness to get at the real work of carving, the tools must be left untouched until every possible means has been explored for visualising the whole finished work inside the block in front of you.

With animate objects—cats, portraits, heads etc.—the preparatory stage of the work is more difficult as such things resent being enclosed within a 'visualising box' for any length of time. The usual solution to this problem is to work from drawings or rough sketch models in clay or plasticine. This latter approach is really positive as it allows for a preliminary excursion through the main forms without inhibiting the carver's final interpretation of them. The practice is condemned where it leads to slavish copying and it becomes really tedious when a craftsman carver in wood or stone is required to make an exact copy or enlargement of a clay model provided by an artist.

There is no easy solution to the business of drawing for people who are shy of the work, inexperienced in it or—and this possibly concerns the majority of people outside the hard core of professional artists—who have had their confidence in their capacity as draughtsmen destroyed by bad teaching. Drawing is, in the end, only a matter of making a permanent record of what we see. If we see accurately then we can draw, but, returning to Henry Moore's words on page 28, we find that learning to see accurately, in three-dimensions at least, is a lifetime's work. He supports his argument with Rembrandt's series of self-portraits, and I have experienced myself the uncanny sensation of reaching forward to lift a figure out of a sketch by this artist. Rembrandt was not a sculptor, but in his drawing he reveals an amazing grasp of solid form. In a few strokes he conveyed everything—weight, distance, cross-section, curvature and feel.

We can only try and enjoy making progress. Half closing the eyes is a help in simplifying what we are looking at, cutting out the clutter of accidental lights, darks or obtrusive bits of colour. Looking through a small square or rectangular hole cut in a post card is another help in isolating images and visualising space or solidity by revealing the true lines of perspective.

Finally, to round off these remarks on observing and making three-dimensional forms, we could return profitably for a few moments to the writings of Bernard Berenson from whom I have taken the word 'tactile'. The book mentioned in the footnote on page 25 commences with an essay on Giotto (1267–1336) who was the first painter in Florence to move away from the decorative illustrative paintings of the Byzantine and Medieval periods to a more convincing figurative imagery. This movement gained momentum with the subsequent Florentine painters—and sculptors—up to Michelangelo after which it became somewhat decadent.

Berenson begins his essay with a brief analysis of what he regards as the essence of the craft of figurative painting which was the dominant preoccupation of the Florentine school. He suggests that sight alone gives no accurate sense of the third dimension and that in infancy, long before we are conscious of the process, the sense of touch, helped on by muscular sensations of movement, teaches us to appreciate depth, the third dimension, both in objects and in space.

He then goes on to reveal that after a long study of Florentine paintings he began to realise that the only pictures that 'affected him lastingly' were those in which the artist had succeeded in giving 'tactile values to visual* impressions' or, as he also put it, providing him with 'the illusion of varying muscular sensations corresponding to the various projections of the figure'. The emphasis here is upon those which *affected him lastingly*—the effect of Degas' Dancer on myself—for he had seen and enjoyed many other pictures from all the generations prior to Giotto which attractively told their stories *as illustrations* but 'lost all higher value the moment the message had been delivered'.

In ordinary circumstances Berenson felt that 'we have considerable difficulty in skimming off tactile values and by the time they have reached our consciousness, they have lost much of their strength. Obviously, the artist who gives us these values more rapidly than the object itself gives them, gives us the pleasures consequent upon a more vivid realisation of the object'—'a higher coefficient of reality to the object represented' and 'an exhilarating sense of increased capacity in the observer.'

With all this I agree entirely, despite the fact that the remarks were sparked off by a study of painting. Everywhere about us, in buildings, offices, schools, shops or colleges and among the objects made by craftsmen of all kinds, is evidence of a peculiar deadness caused by lack of attention to the tactile or three-dimensional aspect of the arts. As carvers we have unlimited scope and sadly little competition. The world is hungry for beauty and has lost sight of what was achieved in this respect during the Creation. With our mallets and gouges we can each do a little to make good the loss. Praise the Lord for the opportunity and the excitement of it all!

*Not 'visual' but 'retinal' in the original.

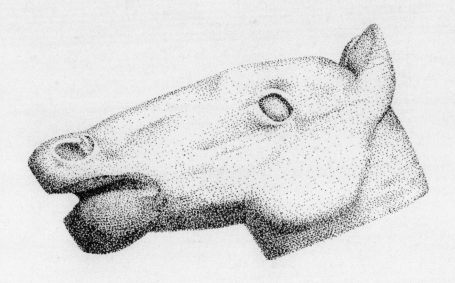

'The Blood Horse' by John Skeaping.
(Tate Gallery, London)

SAFETY

With a block of wood fixed firmly on the bench, a gouge in one hand and a mallet in the other it seems quite impossible to injure oneself. Yet, in every workshop accidents do happen and regrettably mine has been no exception. Only a month or two ago my son jabbed a gouge through to the bone of his forefinger. The previous week another workshop nearby was saved from burning by a passer-by at 2 am detecting the smell of smouldering wood. Then, apparently, John Skeaping's grandfather cut off his thumb with a gouge and died from the injury.

Why? In each of these three cases investigation reveals that for a moment the ordinary and sensible ways of working had been abandoned. My son was holding a heavy carving in one hand and prising off some firmly attached bark with a gouge in the other; the smouldering fire was caused by self-ignition in a mountain of wet elm shavings produced by an overheated router; Skeaping's grandfather was drunk and the story goes that he attempted to mend his thumb with glue and shavings.

So, whenever a tool is used for the wrong purpose, for the right purpose in the wrong way, when the operator is not fully in control of his faculties—perhaps only through tiredness—or where the workshop is thoroughly messy, something is likely to go wrong. Consciousness of these dangers seems to me to be the only realistic safeguard. However, self-ignition can occur in relatively tidy workshops, even where there is no smoking. Rags used for linseed oil are a recognized hazard of this kind and any volatile glues or varnishes should be used with care.

With children the circumstances are different. The majority of hand tools are too big for their bodies to manage and with machine tools their experience of life in general is too short to enable them to envisage the

129

amount of damage that can be done by an instrument which, when used correctly, appears to work so easily. But, despite the possible risks, I am convinced that as soon as they are beyond babyhood children should be encouraged to make things and to use a workshop without anxiety or continual supervision.

If the 'right tool' is too big for a child to handle there is usually a substitute that will do the work quite well. For instance, hacksaws can cut wood as effectively as metal and a child soon learns that it is more satisfying to use a tool like this, which he can cope with, than to struggle with a 24 inch cross-cut or a heavy tenon saw which, in any case, he is certain to ruin. Small gouges, mallets, hammers and block planes are made for detailed cabinet work and the traditional hand-drill has surely never caused an injury since it was invented. With real tools such as these clearly set aside for them children quickly develop confidence, sense and the feel for correct usage and maintenance of tools. This growth seems to me to be as important as learning to read or write and the best prevention of accidents—now or in later life.

BIBLIOGRAPHY

Trees and Timber : General

Edlin, H. L., TREES, WOODS AND MAN, Collin's New Naturalist Series, 1956 with many reprints. History of forests, uses, crafts and individual tree studies. Excellent illustrations.

Edlin, H. L., THE LIVING FORESTS, Thames and Hudson, 1958. A history of trees and timber. Excellent reading, no illustrations.

Forest Products and Laboratories Division, Ottawa, CANADIAN WOODS, THEIR PROPERTIES AND USES, 1951.

Forest Products Research, HANDBOOK OF HARDWOODS, H.M.S.O., 1956. Full descriptions of 161 timbers with notes on a further 64. Replaces EMPIRE TIMBERS (last revised 1945) and HOME GROWN TIMBERS (last revised 1941). Descriptions cover defects, durability and workability.

THE INTERNATIONAL BOOK OF WOOD, Foreword by Hugh Johnson, Mitchell Beazley Publishers, London, 1976 and 1979. Substantial collection of illustrations and information on past and present constructional uses; furniture; the arts associated with wood; the nature of wood, its growth, distribution and types with colour illustrations of samples.

Record, S. and Hess, R., TIMBERS OF THE NEW WORLD, Yale and Oxford, 1943.

Rendle, B., WORLD TIMBERS (3 vols), Benn, 1969. Reprints of articles from the extinct journal WOOD. Good colour reproductions of each timber described. Vol. I; Europe and Africa. Vol. II; Americas and West Indies. Vol. III; Asia, Australia and New Zealand.

Rodgers, J., THE ENGLISH WOODLAND, Batsford, 1941. A regional survey of woods and forests, with history, folk lore etc.

Yale School of Forestry, PROPERTIES AND USES OF TROPICAL WOODS, (Tropical Woods Nos 95–103) 1949–55.

Timber : Technical

British Standards Institution, NOMENCLATURE OF COMMERCIAL TIMBERS
INCLUDING SOURCES OF SUPPLY, London, 1955. British Standards Nos
589 and 881.

Forest Products Research Laboratory, THE AIR SEASONING OF SAWN
TIMBER, (Leaflet No. 21) HMSO 1964.

Harris, P., A HANDBOOK OF WOODCUTTING, Forest Products Research
Laboratory, HMSO, 1946.

Schwankl, Dr. A., BARK, Thames and Hudson, 1956. Translation by
H. L. Edlin. Useful for recognition of types, health and disease as well
as for knowledge of the function etc.

US Department of Agriculture, WOOD HANDBOOK. (Handbook No. 72),
The Forest Products Laboratories, Madison, Wisconsin, 1955.

Willis, W. E., TIMBER FROM FOREST TO CONSUMER, Benn, 1968. Describes
the international timber trade—importing, grading, measurement,
maintenance, preservation and properties.

Timbers : Identification

Edlin, H. L., WHAT WOOD IS THAT? Stobart and Son, 1977. (First
edition. Thames and Hudson, 1969). A system of identification based
on fourteen aspects such as colour, smell, hardness, weight, pores etc.
Contains 40 samples of veneers.

See above: Rendle, WORLD TIMBERS and THE INTERNATIONAL BOOK OF
WOOD.

Trees : Identification

Clapham, A., THE OXFORD BOOK OF TREES. 1975. Excellent paintings (by
Barbara Nicholson) of general views, details, bark etc. and with much
additional information—equally well illustrated—about woodland
scenery and the habits of trees.

Phillips, R., TREES IN BRITAIN, EUROPE AND NORTH AMERICA, Pan Books,
1978. Recognition by single leaves, leaves grouped according to
shape, fruits, flowers, winter silhouettes and bark. All in good colour;
224 pages.

Tools : History, Uses, Maintenance

Blandford, P., COUNTRY CRAFT TOOLS, David and Charles, 1974. First class account of the tools our predecessors—and some contemporaries—have used for building and the manufacture of everything required by rural and farming communities. Illustrated with clear line drawings.

Goodman, W. L., THE HISTORY OF WOODWORKING TOOLS, Bell, 1964. Chapters devoted to the chief types with bibliography and museum list. Standard reference.

Jackson, A. and Day, D., THE COMPLETE BOOK OF TOOLS, Michael Joseph, 1978. Brief notes on the construction and uses of about 600 tools for all trades including modern power hand tools. Clear illustrations.

Salaman, R. A., DICTIONARY OF TOOLS (USED IN THE WOODWORKING AND ALLIED TRADES, c 1700–1970 AD), Allen and Unwin, 1975. Over 500 pages of superb reference, fully and beautifully illustrated with line drawings and reproductions of contemporary catalogue engravings. Expensive but invaluable.

Watson, A., THE VILLAGE BLACKSMITH, Thomas Crowell, N.Y., 1977. Beautifully illustrated. Gives a clear insight into the manufacture of small tools and devices from wrought iron.

Woodcrafts

Edlin, H. L., WOODLAND CRAFTS OF BRITAIN, David and Charles, 1973. (First published 1949). An account of the traditional uses of trees and timbers in the British countryside, arranged in chapters devoted to each type of tree.

Langsner, D., COUNTRY CRAFTS, Rodale Press, Penn., 1978. A full and practical account of splitting, fencemaking, gatemaking, toolhandling, rough furniture making and many other processes associated with woodlands—including rough hewn bowls.

Rose, W., THE VILLAGE CARPENTER, Cambridge, 1937; E. P. Publishing, 1973. Rich personal experience. See text quotes, pages 54 and 60.

Woodcarving : Traditional Methods

Christensen, E., EARLY AMERICAN WOODCARVING, Dover, 1972. Reprint of a book published by World Publications Co. in 1952. Ornaments, portraits, figures, animals etc.

Gross, C., THE TECHNIQUE OF WOOD SCULPTURE, Vista House, N.Y., 1957. A serious and chatty account by an experienced artist. Excellent list of exotic woods.

Hasluck, P. N., MANUAL OF TRADITIONAL WOODCARVING, Dover, 1977. Reprint of a book of traditional methods and patterns first published by Cassell in 1911.

Jack, G., WOODCARVING, Pitman/Taplinger, N.Y., 1978. A standard work since 1903, and one of the famous series of craftbooks edited by W. R. Lethaby. Many reprints over the years.

Naylor, R., WOODCARVING TECHNIQUES, Batsford, 1979. A typical example of many recent handbooks. Contains useful practical tips.

Reference

Corkhill, T., A GLOSSARY OF WOOD, Stobart and Son, 1979. Reprint of the fullest reference book on the subject. Contains 10,000 definitions with diagrams.

LIST OF SUPPLIERS

Carving Tools : Retailers

Alan Holtham, The Old Stores Turnery, Wistaston Road, Willaston, Nantwich, Cheshire. (0270 67010)

Avery Knight Ltd., 106 Walcot Street, Bath, BA1 5BG. (0225 66294)

Roger's, 47 Walsworth Road, Hitchin, Herts. (0462 4177)

Alec Tiranti Ltd., 21 Goodge Place, London W1. Or by mail: 70 High St., Theale, Reading, Berks.

Massy Wykeham Ltd., 5th Floor, 26 Cross St., Manchester M2 AW. (061 834 5022)

Carving Tools : Manufacturers

Carl Heidtmann, 563 Remscheid—Hasten, Unterholterfelder Str. 46, West Germany.

Ashley Iles (Edge Tools) Ltd., Fenside, East Kirkby, Spilsby, Lincs. (079 03 372)

Henry Taylor, The Forge, Lowther Road, Owlerton, Sheffield S6 2DR (0742 340282)

General Tools : Addresses for Catalogues etc.

Benmail Supplies, Station Road, St. Georges, Weston-super-Mare, Avon BS22 0XL.

135

Buckingham Tool Co., PO Box 25, Crondall, Farnham, Surrey.

Peter Child, The Old Hyde, Little Yeldham, Halstead, Essex. (0787 237291) (Pyrographic equipment, waxes, sealers, wood stopping for cracks, discs of assorted wood. Woodturning specialist.)

James Neill (Sheffield) Ltd., Napier Street, Sheffield S11 8HB. (0742 71281) (Files, Eclipse saw sharpeners.)

Record Ridgway Tools Ltd., Parkway Works, Sheffield S9 3BL. (0742 448066)

Spear and Jackson (Tools) Ltd., St. Pauls Road, Wednesbury, Staffordshire WS10 9RA.

Stanley Tools Ltd., Woodside, Sheffield S3 GPD.

U.S.A. : Retailers

Art Consultants, 100 E. 7th St., New York, NY 10009

Brookstone Co. Dept. C., 4 Brookstone Buildings, Peterborough, New Hampshire 03458

Buck Brothers, Inc., Millbury, Mass. 01527

Craftsman Wood Service Co., 2127 Mary St., Chicago, Ill. 60608 (tools and wood)

Dirty Rainbow Artists' Materials, 2514 Durant Ave., Berkeley, Ca., 94704

Ettl Studios, Inc., Ettl Art Center, Greenwich, Conn. 06830

Frank Mittermeier, Inc., 3566 East Tremont Avenue, Bronx, New York, NY 10465

Sculpture Associates, Ltd., 114 East 25th St., New York, NY 10010

Sculpture House, Inc., 38 East 30th St., New York, NY 100016

Sculpture Services, Inc., 9 East 19th St., New York, NY 10003

Heidl Slocum Co., Inc., 78–82 Reade St., New York, NY 10008

Jack D. Wolfe Co., 724–734 Meeker Ave., Brooklyn, NY 11222

Woodcraft Supply Corporation, 313 Montvale Avenue, Woburn, Mass. 01801

The following magazines carry advertisements for timber supplies and tools:

CRAFTS. (six issues per year, published by The Crafts Council of Great Britain). 28 Haymarket, London SW1Y 4YZ.

PRACTICAL WOODWORKING. (monthly). IPC Magazines Ltd., King's reach Tower, Stamford Street, London SE1 9LS.

WOODWORKER. (monthly). Model and Allied Publications Ltd., 13–35 Bridge Street, Hemel Hempstead, Herts HP1 1EE.

WOOD AND EQUIPMENT NEWS. (monthly). Westbourne Journals Ltd., Crown House, London Road, Morden, Surrey SM4 5EB.

WORKING WOOD. (four issues per year). Lansdowne Warehouse, Lansdowne Road, Aldershot, Hampshire. (Commenced publication in 1979).

INDEX